The PENTECOSTAL RAPTURE

of the CHURCH of JESUS CHRIST

Jack W. Langford

The PENTECOSTAL RAPTURE

of the CHURCH of JESUS CHRIST

Jack W. Langford

First Edition, 1997
Second, 2007
Third, 2014

Copyright © 2014 by Jack W. Langford

The Pentecostal Rapture of the Church of Jesus Christ
by Jack W. Langford

Printed in the United States of America

ISBN 9781498408301

All rights reserved solely by the author. The author guarantees all contents are original and do not infringe upon the legal rights of any other person or work. No part of this book may be reproduced in any form without the permission of the author. The views expressed in this book are not necessarily those of the publisher.

Permission to quote or reproduce passages from this publication is granted with the stipulations that they are not altered in content, used for profit in any manner and proper citation of the source is given.

Scripture quotations taken from The NEW KING JAMES VERSION. Copyright © 1979, 1980, 1982 by Thomas Nelson, Inc.; and The NEW AMERICAN STABDARD BIBLE. Copyright © 1960, 1962, 1963, 1968, 1971, 1972, 1973, 1975, 1977 by the Lockman Foundation.

www.xulonpress.com

TABLE OF CONTENTS

INTRODUCTION

Chapter One — What is PENTECOST?

Acts 2:1 and 2 17
What is the Real Purpose of the Feast of Pentecost? 19
The New Field of Grain 20
Pentecost is to the Church what Passover was to Israel 24

Chapter Two — PROPHETIC OBSERVATIONS

Prophetic Lessons in the Liturgical Calendar of Israel 27
The Prophets speak of A Future Application of the Feasts 29
Observations by Bible Teachers 32

Chapter Three — IS THE CHURCH TYPIFIED IN THE HEBREW SCRIPTURES?

Objection 36
Positive Answers 38
More Examples 51

Chapter Four — IMPORTANT CLARIFICATIONS

How Many Feasts Are There? 54
The Important Arrangement of Pentecost 59
Relationship of *Shavuot* to the Law 65
In Summary 67

Chapter Five — PRELUDE TO PENTECOST

Offering of the Wave-sheaf of Firstfruits 70
Various Names for Pentecost 72
"Christ the Firstfruits" 74
"Counting of Days" 76
Significance of the Number 50 77

Chapter Six — the PARAKLETOS OF PENTECOST

Uniqueness of Pentecost 79
The Parakletos of Pentecost 80
The Administration of the Spirit 83
"When the Day of Pentecost was *Fully* Come" 86
The "New Grain Offering" 87

Chapter Seven — PROPHETIC ASPECT OF PENTECOST

Prophetic Character derived from the Wave-sheaf at Passover 92
The Prophetic Application of this Feast to the Church by the
Apostle Paul —
    I Corinthians 15:20 and 23 94
    Leviticus 23:7; Romans 8:11 and 23 99
    Romans 15:15 and 16 101
    Further Confirmations from Paul 102

Chapter Eight — FULL PURPOSE OF PENTECOST

Why was the Church Born on Pentecost? 106
"If The *Firstfruit* is Holy, the *Lump* is also Holy" 109
Three Areas of Example 110
On Pentecost A.D. 30, A Preliminary Fourth Example 112
Both Christ and the Church "Raptured" 113

Table Of Contents

Chapter Nine—ENOCH and PENTECOST

The Translation of Enoch 115
Enoch and the Rapture 116
Enoch and Prophecy 118
Enoch and the Mysteries 119
Enoch and Pentecost 121

Chapter Ten—THE APPROACHING PENTECOST

A Unique Feature of Passover 124
Time of the Rapture of the Church 126
The Passover which Closed the Age of Law 127
The Antitypical Pentecost which Closes the Age of Grace 130

Chapter Eleven—DISPENSATIONS and PENTECOST

Dispensational Comparisons and Contrasts 133
From the Letters of Paul—The History of Each Age 136
Romans 11:15–27 139
The Exact Close of Each Dispensation 142
How will the Gentile Age Close? 143

Chapter Twelve—PERFECTION OF PENTECOST

The "Counting of Days" 146
Two Human Blunders 148
The "Divine, Perfect Consummation of Time" 150
"The Dispensation of the Fullness of Times" 153
Fullness or Completion 155
The Restoration of Israel 157

ADDENDUM

20 REASONS FOR THE PRETRIBULATIONAL RAPTURE OF THE CHURCH

Defining the Rapture 161
Dispensational Distinctions 162
REASON NO.—
I   The Rapture is Missing from the Resurrection Prophesies of the Hebrew Scriptures 164
II   The Church is not in the Prophesied 70 Weeks of Daniel 165
III   The Rapture of the Church is not found in Matthew 3, 13, 24 or 25 166
IV   The Church was a "Mystery," not previously revealed 167
V   The "Mystery" Character of the Rapture Itself 168
VI   The Unique promises of John 14 Compared with 1 Thessalonians 4 169
VII The Unique Presentation of the Church Into Heaven 170
VIII The Restrainer Removed Prior to the Day of the Lord 171
IX   The Threefold Order of the Resurrection of the Righteous 174
X   The problem of Who Will Furnish the Kingdom—If Both Events Happen Simultaneously 177

THE FIVE CONFLICTS
XI The Conflict of Economies 180
XII The Conflict of Buildings 181
XIII The Conflict of Hopes 181
XIV The Conflict of "Grace" versus "Wrath" 182
XV The Conflict of Reigns 183

THE FIVE CONFIRMATIONS
XVI The Great Tribulation is Jewish in Nature—Not Church-Oriented 184
XVII The Great Tribulation "Saints" are Not Church Saints 185
XVIII The Great Tribulation is the "Time of Jacob's Trouble," Not the Church's Trouble 186
XIX In The Great Tribulation, the "Woman" of God's Favor Is Israel, Not the Church 187
XX The Great Tribulation Spells the Doom of Apostate Christendom 188
In Conclusion 189

INTRODUCTION

There were two preliminary subjects that led me to this present volume which I have called *The Pentecostal Rapture of the Church of Jesus Christ*. Each subject brought me progressively closer to the necessity of a carefully detailed look at the scriptural revelations concerning—what Jewish teachers have themselves described as a "mystery Feast"—Shavuot, better known to us as Pentecost.

First of all, many years ago I was challenged to make an investigation of the Passover Feast and its relationship to the death of Jesus Christ as described in the New Testament. This began with a study of the Passover's scriptural chronology as revealed in the Law of Moses. The study continued by looking at the historical practices regarding the Passover celebration, both in the rest of the Hebrew Scriptures and in the uninspired traditions of Judaism. Finally, my study focused upon the drama surrounding the death of Jesus Christ, which was obviously unfolding upon the backdrop of the Passover subject as revealed in the Greek Scriptures, primarily in the four Gospel accounts.

The reason for my focus upon this area of study was that biblical critics, infidels and agnostics have long claimed that one of the foremost inaccuracies in the Bible is its contradictory record concerning the day upon which Christ died. Even some Bible scholars have said that the problem appeared unsolvable.

However, I found that not only was the apparent problem solvable, but the scriptural solution leaves both the critic and the scoffer in embarrassment. You can read about this in my book, *The Day Christ Died as Our Passover*.

Second, this study of the Passover subject, with its joyful solution, happened to lead me into another area of realization concerning an additional vital question which has developed immensely in our own time. This has to do with the questions centered on the subject of the bodily resurrection of the righteous. Many have wondered if all the righteous of all the ages are to be resurrected together, or if there are stages to it. Naturally, some might wonder what the connection is between the Passover and the resurrection subject. The association of the Passover with the resurrection subject is the fact that a special Offering during the Passover Feast was the Wave-sheaf of Firstfruits, which the apostle Paul told us in 1 Corinthians 15:20 and 23 was the first "order" of the resurrection of the righteous. Paul further stated emphatically that this Offering has reference to Christ's resurrection from the dead. Furthermore, this Offering is the actual basis for understanding and interpreting the later Offering of the two Wave-loaves of Bread at the Feast of Pentecost. In the revealed celebration of these two Offerings there is an actual countdown of "days" and "weeks" between them. The first is the basis for the observance of the second. This second Offering would, therefore, represent the second "order" of the resurrection of the righteous. The apostle Paul designated the second "order" as "those who are Christ's at His coming." Then Paul continued to describe a third "order" in this resurrection of the righteous.

Therefore, back in 1982, I realized a need for a second extensive study on the overall parallel between what has been called "the Three Harvest Feasts of Israel" and the three "orders" or stages in the resurrection of the righteous. You can read about this study in my book, *The Threefold Order of the Resurrection of the Righteous*. I believe you will find this to be very helpful in seeing the overall plan of God concerning the resurrection of His saints beautifully laid out in simplicity and order. It is also important to see the distinction between the second and third "orders." The resurrection and Rapture of the Church is a separate event from the resurrection of the Old Testament and Tribulation saints which composes the last or third "order." Indeed, if there are three "orders" to the resurrection of the righteous, and they are typified by the three Harvest Feasts of Israel, then that middle Feast (Pentecost) would typify *the resurrection and*

Rapture of the Church of Jesus Christ. This is clearly separate and distinct from the resurrection of the Old Testament and Tribulation saints.

Now, this brings us to the present volume which I have named — *The Pentecostal Rapture of the Church of Jesus Christ*. Herein one must walk very carefully. Most Bible teachers have long recognized the prophetic nature of the Feasts in Israel's calendar. I will point out in this study that the Hebrew prophets themselves spoke of future aspects regarding the Feast of Passover and the Feast of Tabernacles. In addition to that, the apostle Paul told us plainly in Colossians 2:16 and 17, ". . . regarding a festival or a new moon or Sabbaths, which are a *shadow* of things to come. . . ." Because of this, many teachers have sought to find a future celebration which would fit the Rapture of the Church. There has, no doubt, been a lot of confusion and misuse of Scripture in this area.

I know of other Bible teachers who have long suspected that the Feast of Pentecost somehow better fits an application to the Church and its ultimate destiny, but they have hesitated to make that application because of certain unanswered questions. I believe, in this study, you will find the right answers to these questions!

Certain features of this investigation will demonstrate that Pentecost is the only Feast day on Israel's liturgical calendar which is looked upon as a *"mystery"* Feast, and is most certainly identified with *Gentile* believers. We shall see that there are actually many other features about this Feast which typify the present Church dispensation. Last, but not least, I have also found that this is the only Feast on the liturgical calendar which could typify the Rapture and at the very same time not be subject to the error of "date-setting" in terms of its prophetic fulfillment. In other words, we shall find that Pentecost actually *avoids* for us the necessity of specifying a date for the Rapture of the Church. In addition, we shall find that it does not violate the principle doctrine of *"imminence"* in connection with the expectancy of the Rapture.

This study will also answer those who have strong reservations about finding any typologies in the Hebrew Scriptures concerning the Church of Jesus Christ.

Obviously, if the second "order" in the resurrection of the righteous is to be found typified by the special Offering on the Day of Pentecost of the two Wave-loaves, which is offered just exactly like the *sample* Wave-sheaf at Passover, then the Day of Pentecost itself must be typical of much more than just "the birthday of the Church." Indeed, we shall find that this special Offering signifies the resurrection and/or Rapture of the Church, itself! In fact, I believe it would be better stated that the Church of Jesus Christ was simply born on the very Feast day which primarily typifies the Church's resurrection and Rapture into heaven.

Now I hope I have whetted your appetite to read this material. I believe you will find that it is honoring to our Savior, the Lord Jesus Christ, and is certainly spiritually invigorating, especially in these very last days. Our departure is just around the corner. Are you prepared for it? If so, let's go—

One additional note—

As you have already seen in this study, I am going to be capitalizing the various designations for the Feasts and special Offerings and the word Rapture. This is for emphasis' sake. I am also going to be capitalizing the word *Church* because I want to stress the exclusive and unique position of "the Church which is Christ's body" apart from all other churches which men have built. Sadly, it is true that the vast majority of real Christians are carnally mixed into the various denominations and sects of Christendom. However, the Church of Jesus Christ is not "Christendom." It consists of only those individuals "born again" by the Spirit of God and "baptized into the one body—the Church which is Christ's body" (1 Cor. 12:13 and Eph. 1:22, 23). "Christendom" is not going to be Raptured to meet Christ in the air. Only those who are members of "the Church which is His body" are going to be "snatched away." Make no mistake about it, "Christendom" (alias, "Mystery Babylon") is going right straight into the "the Great Tribulation"! Not so, with the collective "body of Christ"! Consequently, many of Christendom's churches will have absentees, some more, some less, at the time of the Rapture.

Chapter One

What is PENTECOST?

Acts 2:1 and 2

*"When the day of Pentecost had fully come,
they were all with one accord in one place.
And suddenly there came a sound from heaven, . . ."*

As you can see by the title of this book, and by the simplicity of the passage quoted above, this is going to be a Bible study focusing upon the subject and meaning of the Day of Pentecost. In the narrowest sense, therefore, we will be studying Acts two, verses one and two. That may sound over simplistic to many Bible teachers and students. However, I believe you are going to find this very enlightening because, more often than not, God uses the simple things of His revelation to both illuminate the humble and to confound "the wise" in this world (1 Cor. 1:18–25). Actually, we shall discover that a prophetic aspect of the truth of Acts 2:1 and 2 is going to be repeated at the very end of this present Church Age. In other words, when the antitypical *"Pentecost has fully come,"* there will be *"a sound from heaven"* and once again all the members of the body of Christ will find themselves *"with one accord in one place."* Of course, I am making reference to the Rapture of the Church as described in 1 Thessalonians 4:15–17.

Many are curious, I am sure, as to just what the Day of Pentecost has to do with the subject of the Rapture of the Church. As we study this Feast day carefully and in some detail, we shall see, according to the Pauline revelation, that *Pentecost* was not merely the birthday of the Church of Jesus Christ, but it also was a God-given type of the *Rapture* of the Church. The apostle Paul spoke of the future prophetic aspect of this Feast day very discreetly. We shall discover that *Pentecost,* according to Paul's revelation, stands as emblematic of the second "order" (1 Cor. 15:23) of the resurrection of the righteous, i.e., the Rapture of the Church. In addition, we shall find out that the subject of the Feast of Pentecost has been impregnated by the Holy Spirit of inspiration with a beautiful and complete picture characterizing aspects of the Church of Jesus Christ and the subject of its resurrection and ascension which take place in an important and clear sequence of dispensational time. I have found that the vast majority of prophetic Bible teachers have been either negligent or else oblivious of the last of these facts.

One writer has stated the following concerning the subject of the pretribulational Rapture teaching—"The evidence has been sifted, the Scriptures that purportedly support pretribulationism proven scanty, and the arguments made. I believe there are no *hidden veins* in traditional pretribulationism yet to be mined" (Marvin Rosenthal, *The Pre-Wrath Rapture of The Church,* 1990, page 33). It is my privilege to present to you in this Bible study many *"hidden veins"* to be mined, which I believe are untouchable and irrefutable concerning the doctrine of the Rapture of the Church prior to the occurrence of "the Seventieth Week of Daniel" (Dan. 9:24 and 27).

Next to the glorious salvation experience of a repentant sinner trusting in the blood atonement provided through our Lord Jesus Christ, there is no subject to thrill the soul with more longing and anticipation than the "goal" of the "upward call" (Philip. 3:14 and Col. 1:5) of the Church of Jesus Christ. Any believer who becomes too self-centered and distracted with worldly attainment, will not only lose that purifying and glorious purpose for living, but will also lose rewards when standing before the Savior.

What is the Real Purpose of the Feast of Pentecost?

Most Bible students should know that the Church of Jesus Christ was born on the Day of Pentecost, as recorded for us in the early chapters of the book of Acts (the extreme dispensationalists, to the contrary, not withstanding). This was the day and the hour on which the promised baptism of the Holy Spirit first took place (Luke 24:49; Acts 1:3; 2:1, 2). The Holy Spirit took up His residence upon the earth in the midst of His people, baptizing them "into one body" and forming a "new man" (1 Cor. 12:13 and Eph. 2:15). This was not a haphazard accident of scheduling on God's part. That idea should be the farthest thing from anyone's mind. Though this is what happened on the Day of Pentecost at the beginning of this Christian Dispensation, yet it does not tell us the full and real purpose of the Feast of Pentecost.

Most Christians I have talked to really don't know what the Day of Pentecost is and many Bible teachers themselves only have a vague idea as to why God chose that particular day as the birthday for the Church. In our world today, those who have carnally named themselves "Pentecostals" are probably the most ignorant about just exactly what the Day of Pentecost was and is! We all know that a lot of beautiful things happened on Pentecost, like the establishment of miraculous gifts of the Spirit, and the beginning of the Church as a new institution—but that does not tell us the literal, original purpose this Feast day actually represented.

Read these next statements carefully because herein is embedded the basis for the prophetic aspect of truth conveyed by the Feast of Pentecost. In its historical setting, as given by God to Moses, Pentecost was simply and essentially a *Harvest* Feast. This Feast actually was the ceremonial commemoration of the *early summer harvest* of the grain fields which would occur in the Land of Promise. The Feast day celebrates the spring or early summer harvest. The first Hebrew name given in the Law for this particular Feast was *Hag ha-Katatzin*, which means "Feast of the Harvest" (Exo. 23:16). Some of later years would say *Hag ha-Katsir*, which simply means "Harvest Festival." This was Pentecost's first and foremost purpose as far as the nation of Israel was concerned.

Now, however, at the beginning of the book of Acts, God specifically chose this early Harvest Feast as the day upon which He was going to create a whole *new* "field" of grain—a field that would spread way beyond the borders of Israel to actually engulf all nations on the face of the whole earth. Remember also that God specifically designated the special Offering to be made on this day as "*a new grain offering*" (Lev. 23:16). No doubt, in the understanding of the children of Israel, this designation had reference to the fact that this grain was "new" in the sense of it being the first grain for the New Year on Israel's liturgical calendar. However, since this Feast was also designated as one of "the Appointed Times of the Lord" (literal trans., Lev. 23:1, NASB), and since this Feast was "a shadow" of things to come (Col. 2:17), we might also understand that the "time" it foreshadowed was the present "Dispensation of the Grace of God" (Eph. 3:2). Of course, we will explore this more carefully as we move throughout this study. Nevertheless, on the Day of Pentecost of Acts 2:1, when the "*New Grain Offering*" was being "waved" up in the air, the "*one New Man*" (Eph. 2:15) had its actual beginning.

For a moment let us trace the origins and early growth of this "new grain field" or "one New Man" from John's Gospel account, the book of Acts, and the epistles of Paul—as this particular field of grain is primarily going to include and encompass believing Gentile people from all over the world.

The New Field of Grain

You no doubt remember that on the day when Christ made His formal entrance into Jerusalem, which in Christendom is called, "the Triumphal Entrance," He also spoke about His death as being the basis of a whole new harvest of souls. In John 12:20–26 we have this very important and amazing revelation—

> Now there were certain Greeks among those who came up to worship at the Feast [Passover]. Then they came to Philip, who was from Bethsaida of Galilee, and asked him, 'Sir, we would see Jesus.' Philip came and told Andrew, and in turn Andrew and Philip told

Jesus. But Jesus answered them, saying, 'The hour has come that the Son of Man should be glorified. Most assuredly, I say to you, *unless a grain of wheat falls into the ground and dies, it abides alone; but if it dies, it produces much grain.*'

Now this is an amazing revelation, primarily because it has a reflection upon God's program with the Gentile people. No doubt, during Christ's earthly ministry, on certain rare occasions, He spoke with Gentile people. However, this was not at all His primary audience. In fact, He had carefully instructed the apostles "Do not go into the way of the Gentiles, and do not enter a city of the Samaritans. But go rather to the lost sheep of the house of Israel" (Matt. 10:5, 6). This is probably why Philip did not immediately introduce these Gentiles to Jesus. Rather, he thought it best to consult with Andrew. Then both of them went to Jesus to see what He would say and do.

What Christ said to Philip and Andrew may seem hard to comprehend at first because it most certainly postpones His dealing with Gentile people on a public basis until a later date. In the Law of Moses Gentiles were allowed to come to Jerusalem to observe the Jewish Feasts. That is why these Grecians were present in Jerusalem at this time. However, in the Temple services there was a "middle wall of partition" which separated them from the native Jewish people (Ephesians 2:11–18). It was strictly forbidden for any uncircumcised Gentiles to cross that wall, even with the threat of death.

In this particular incident, recounted for us in John's Gospel, it becomes evident that Christ was stating that the time for Gentiles to be received in a place of nearness to God would be after the *"the grain of wheat falls into the ground and dies"* — that is, after the death of Jesus Christ and not before. In other words, Christ is saying that His death would actually produce much fruit — especially among the Gentile people. In reality, it would be the gospel message of the actual death, burial and resurrection of Jesus Christ which would furnish the *seed to be sown* by the apostles and disciples throughout all the world, not only in Israel. In this regard, we note that the "Great Commission" of Christ after His resurrection, is — "Go therefore and make disciples *of all nations . . .* Go into *all the world* and preach the gospel to every creature . . . and that repentance and remission of sins should be preached in His name *to all nations*, beginning at Jerusalem" (Matt. 28:19; Mark 16:16 and Luke 24:47).

In Acts chapter one, verse eight, Luke recorded the precise order for this ministry to be executed. Christ said just before His ascension—

> But you shall receive power when the Holy Spirit has come upon you; and you shall be witnesses to Me [1] in Jerusalem, [2] and in all Judea [3] and Samaria, [4] and to the end of the earth.

And this is precisely how the gospel ministry was carried out. On the Day of Pentecost, when the disciples had received power from the Holy Spirit, Peter and the other apostles first began to preach this gospel message to the Jewish people.

Pentecost then became the **beginning** planting time for this new grain field. Christ had carefully instructed the apostles that they were to wait until the coming of the Holy Spirit upon them. This happened at the Harvest celebration of Pentecost. Only then were they to go out and preach with spiritual power "repentance and remission of sins in His name to all nations, **beginning** in Jerusalem" (Luke 24:47). After being "filled with the Holy Spirit," Peter, indeed, began to break up the fallow ground in the hearts of many Jews from all over the world who had gathered there. The apostles had to virtually "dig about" this hard hearted nation, and then "fertilize it" with the life giving message of the gospel (see Luke 13:6–9). The message soon filled all Judea. Though many were saved, sad to say, the Jewish religious and national leaders remained adamantly against Christ. This would become increasingly evident as time progressed, and consequently there loomed on the near horizon the prophesied destruction of Jerusalem.

After receiving severe persecution from their own Jewish brethren, the disciples were led on to others. Acts 8 records for us the Holy Spirit's leading a move of the ministry of the gospel into the area of Samaria.

Then in Acts 9, God saved the young rabbi named Saul, who had been a foremost antagonist against the faith, and specifically revealed that he would be sent to the Gentile people (Acts 9:15). As in confirmation of this new direction in the proclamation of the gospel, in Acts 10 God pointedly directed the apostle Peter to first go to the Gentile people with the gospel message. These first Gentile converts also had a "Pentecostal experience" of the baptism of the Holy Spirit with the manifestation of the miraculous gift of tongues just as did the Jewish disciples "at the first" (Acts 11:15 and 16).

Then, after Saul's (whose name was changed to Paul) first missionary journey, it was proclaimed "that He [God] had opened the door of faith *to the Gentiles*" (Acts 14:27).

Soon thereafter, James, the Lord's half brother, who was now a responsible leader in Jerusalem, would state "Simon [Peter] has declared how God at the first *visited the Gentiles to take out of them a people for His name*" (Acts 15:14). This would now begin to be the major direction in the Christian communities for a harvesting of world-wide Gentile discipleship.

In 1 Corinthians, chapter 3 verses 6–9, the apostle Paul spoke of the Church of Jesus Christ as a *grain field* in which the ministers labor—

> *I planted* [the gospel], *Apollos watered, but God was causing the growth. So then neither the one who plants nor the one who waters is anything, but God Who causes the growth. Now he who plants and he who waters are one; but each will receive his own reward according to his own labor. For we are God's fellow workers; YOU ARE GOD'S FIELD, God's building.*

No doubt, Paul envisioned the ultimate harvesting of this new "field" when "the *fullness* of the Gentiles has come in" (Rom. 11:25). Of course, I will have much more to say about this later.

In summary—on the day commemorating the early harvest of Israel's fields, God chose to plant and create a different "field" or institution called "the assembly or congregation of Jesus Christ."

The assembly of Israel, which officially had rejected their own Messiah, was going to be set aside in discipline, but in its place a new assembly was created called "one New Man" (Eph. 2:15). From this point forward, God would compose a new field of grain of all those who do believe in Jesus Christ. This is also expressed in terms of God building a new institution with the rejected "Corner Stone" (Acts 4: 11 and 12). The aspect I am stressing here is that God was, as it were, beginning the planting of a new "field" at this time—which finally would have its own special Harvest celebration.

We shall see as we progress in this study, that there is a clear and unmistakable *prophetic* aspect to the Feast of Pentecost as a *Harvest Feast*, which is yet to be fulfilled. The ultimate objective for this new grain field which God began to plant on the Day of Pentecost is in its *future harvest*. Therefore, the real purpose of Pentecost is twofold. First, God chose this Feast as the point in time when He began to plant and build the new "field" or institution. Second, the primary purpose of this "new field" is in its prophetic harvesting. All grain fields are to be harvested. This particular grain field must also be harvested! In fact, if one understands the Feast of Pentecost in its Biblical setting and usage, he will have no problem whatsoever in understanding the doctrine of the pretribulational Rapture of the Church of our Lord Jesus Christ.

So the real and basic purpose of Pentecost is in its nature as a Harvest Feast—and the real question arises—"When will be the actual Harvest which it prefigures?"

Pentecost is to the Church what Passover was to Israel

There are two primary aspects to the Passover event. First, in the history of the nation of Israel, the *Passover* event marked the birth of the nation's existence under the Mosaic Law system, and second, amazing as it may seem, in the process of time the Passover would also mark the termination of the Law system and the setting aside of Israel from a place of favor before God.

As to the first aspect of Passover, all acknowledge that the Passover event served as the birthday for the nation of Israel. Israel was literally born out of the slavery in Egypt, by means of the

Passover sacrifice, to receive a national standing before God. The morning after the Passover Sacrifice the children of Israel began their journey out of Egypt (Exo. 12:29–34 and 40–42). Soon Israel stood at the foot of Mount Sinai to receive her national economy in the form of the Mosaic Law system. Israel lived under that Law system for some fifteen hundred years.

However, we also know that the Passover ceremony was prophetic in nature. The Passover had an actual prophetic fulfillment in the death of the "Lamb of God Who takes away the sins of the world" (John 1:29). In other words, Jesus Christ was clearly designated in the Scriptures as the antitypical Passover Lamb (John 19:36). Paul stated, ". . . Christ, our Passover, was sacrificed for us" (1 Cor. 5:7). In fact, Christ fulfilled every part of the Passover sacrifice to perfection. It was as if the original revelation to Moses about how to observe Passover was actually an amazing blueprint, given fifteen hundred years in advance, as to the exact schedule Christ would follow during the final week of His journey (see my book, *The Day Christ Died as Our Passover*). Christ not only died on the exact schedule of the Passover sacrifice as the world's Passover Lamb but, *in addition,* the Law was then and thereby "nailed to the cross" (Eph. 2:14, 15 and Col. 2:14). Unbelieving national Israel began to be temporarily set aside at that time in the overall perspective of God's dispensational plan.

Therefore, we understand that the Passover served in at least a *twofold* capacity. It served as the birthday for the nation of Israel, but it also marked the termination of Israel's unique position before God at the precise time of Christ's death. The primary prophetic aspect of Passover involved the death of Israel's Messiah. This prophetic aspect of Passover was fulfilled in great detail. However, I say again, this particular Passover also meant the temporary setting aside of Israel's standing before God. Though Israel was virtually born on this Feast Day, yet, in the amazing counsels of God, scriptural revelation began unfolding during the time of the book of Acts to the effect that the Church would eventually come to realize that Israel's actual standing before God was terminated on this very same Feast day. As stated before, that was when "the Law was nailed to the cross."

Now, surprising as it may seem, we shall find that the same principle is true regarding the Church of Jesus Christ relative to the Feast of Pentecost. Like the Passover, the Feast of Pentecost also serves in a *twofold* capacity. It serves not only as the birthday of the Church, yet Pentecost also speaks prophetically of the termination of the Church of Jesus Christ as to its existence here on this earth, as this study is designed to demonstrate. This fact has been largely overlooked by Bible teachers. I can guarantee that if you are patient and are not fearful of a careful and somewhat detailed Bible study, then you will discover many rich blessings as we cover this material.

Chapter Two

PROPHETIC OBSERVATIONS

Prophetic Lessons in The Liturgical Calendar of Israel

Most students of Bible prophecy know that there are very important prophetic messages for God's children in the liturgical calendar of Israel's Feast days. There are several reasons for this. *First* of all, we are specifically told that this is a fact by the apostle Paul. In Paul's epistle to the Colossians, chapter 2 and verses 16 and 17, he stated, concerning the "festivals, new moons and Sabbaths," that they "are a shadow of things to come." This means that God's revealed calendar of the Feasts actually looked forward to the future in fulfillment. *Second*, the Hebrew prophets themselves made future applications from two of the Feasts. We will take a careful look at these statements in a moment. *Third*, there is the very nature of the Feasts themselves. They were designated in the following manner: "Three times a year you shall celebrate a *Feast to Me*" (Exo. 23:14); and again, "Three times a year all your males shall appear *before Jehovah your God in the place which He chooses*" (Exo. 23:17 and Deut. 16:16); in addition, the celebrations of these Feasts are called *"THE APPOINTED TIMES OF THE LORD"* (Lev. 23:4, NASB).

From these statements, four things which God wanted to accentuate become very obvious about these three Feasts.

(1) These Feasts are designated as being *"to God"* and *"before the LORD."* That means, among other things, that God is the

chief participant in the Feasts. It is, as it were, as though God, Himself, sits at the head of the table during the celebrations and the people are appearing to stand before God. This is a very sobering thought. It would most certainly mean that the people's conduct at the Feasts would be very circumspect in light of Who had called them to these Feasts and Who was present.

(2) God designated **the place** where each Feast would be held. This is perfectly proper since God is the originator of the Feasts. This, of course, means that the place is special—God designated the location. Once in the land of Israel, the place where the congregation gathered for the celebration of the Feasts was first at the Tabernacle in Shiloh (Joshua 18:1 and 19:51) and later, in a more permanent way, at the Temple in Jerusalem where God placed His name.

(3) God designated **the time** that the Feasts would be held. Each Feast has a *precise time* schedule when the people would appear before Him. God has a calendar and on His calendar He has designated each of the Feasts in its own proper order of time. It is important to remember that the literal translation of the Hebrew word *mowed, moed* or *mo'adim* (plural) is "appointed time, or times;" hence, these special days and Feasts are properly designated as "the Appointed TIMES of the LORD" (see Lev. 23:2, 4, 37, 44). Many of our newer translations simply translate this word *moed* as "feast" every time it is used. This is not at all accurate. Actually, only three of the "appointed times" (*mo'adim*) on Israel's liturgical calendar were "Feasts" or "Festivals" (Heb. *hag, chag* or *haggim* [plural]). This literal translation of the word *mo'adim* as the "appointed times," by itself, points to a broader application of these events to the overall dispensational *times* of God's dealing with Israel prophetically. In addition, we can add a fourth ingredient—

(4) Exactly what is done at each of these three Feasts is specifically spelled out in the divine revelation given in the Mosaic Law. Each Feast will have its own **particular characteristics** and ritual order. They will not all be the same or identical. They will have different offerings, different ingredients and different purposes.

The celebration of these Feasts would be the central attraction to the whole social and religious life of the nation of Israel. It becomes clear from these passages that these Feasts are not merely times for the cultural fellowship of the households of the children of Israel. They are more specifically representative of "God's Timetable or Calendar" of events. These are designated "times" when Israel would appear before God, Himself. All the liturgical offerings and celebrations done on these Feast days were to be done on this sequential timetable with a view of them being "the appointed Times of the Lord." Therefore, the very nature of these Feasts is *first of all* related to the subject of specific *"Times"* and God's calendar of events. It would therefore only be natural, logical and consistent to also envision in these Feasts a broader historical *time* sequence which they may be signifying and, of course, that is specifically what the Scriptures tell us.

The Prophets Speak of a Future Application of the Feasts

Indeed, and in *second order*, the Hebrew prophets, themselves, would be inspired to see certain future prophetic significances in the *first* and *last* of these three Feasts. We have already stated that the primary fulfillment of the Passover typology took place in regards to the death of Jesus Christ, the antitypical Passover Lamb.

However, Isaiah the prophet also looked forward to a future *"passing over"* wherein God would deliver and preserve Jerusalem and Israel at the very beginning of the Millennial Kingdom (Isa. 31:5). Jeremiah likewise used the symbolism of Israel's being delivered out of Egypt at the original Passover as a picture of the greater future deliverance of Israel from all the nations on the face of the earth (read about it in detail in Jer. 23:7, 8 and 31:31–34). At that future time Jeremiah indicated that Israel would not be looking back to their deliverance out of Egypt (the first Passover) where they received the Old Covenant, but they would be looking forward to their being delivered out of all nations on earth and then receiving the New Covenant. Indeed, at the time of Christ's last Passover celebration, we are told that there was great expectation that at *this Passover* the Kingdom of God would appear and these promises would be fulfilled—see Luke 17:11, 20; 19:11; 22:15-18 and 23:51. These references speak of a prophetic aspect of the Passover event in relationship to the promised Kingdom, which the people expected to be established at that time. I will have more to say about this later. The expected Kingdom deliverance for Israel did not come at that time because the nation of Israel had rejected her King. However, the first and primary prophetic aspect of Passover was spiritual and it did happen at that time.

As to the prophetic aspect of the Feast of Tabernacles, the prophet Zechariah connected it with the acknowledgment of Israel's deliverance, at the beginning of the Kingdom, by all the nations on earth celebrating at the Feast of Tabernacles in Jerusalem. One can read about it in Zech. 14:16–21. This is a fantastic prophecy. What a spectacular celebration that will be! All the nations of earth will be represented at that yearly Feast.

A look at recent history will tell you that a certain Mr. Adolph Hitler had satanic aspirations to be the world's messiah. One prominent historian wrote, ". . . he [Hitler] did not flinch from comparing himself to the Christian savior, . . ." (*Hitler and the Holocaust*, by Robert S. Wistrich, pages 121-123). He openly anticipated and bragged about introducing the "Thousand Year Reich [reign]." I have actually stood before a giant map in Stuttgart, Germany, painted by proud German soldiers depicting the world and all the nations which they had conquered by 1943. Germany was in the center. In addition, I saw a copy of the architectural drawings depicting Nuremberg as the central headquarters for the world. Hitler's grandiose headquarters sat at the head of the magnificent broad pavement leading up to it. Along both sides were the buildings to house the representatives of all nations on earth. And then ten years after the war, I looked around Nuremberg and saw some remaining piles of rubble, a few districts which had not yet been cleared, the several areas of abandoned apartments and homes with nothing but cellars remaining and the lopsided bunker at the main train depot, etc., etc. Where was Hitler? He was in ashes, with a few bones collected by Soviet intelligence. They were only able to identify him by a dental record. Yes, Hitler's grandiose expectations were totally exploded. And the only thing left was the jawbone from which his boastful claims were foolishly and arrogantly made.

Not so, will it be when the Lord Jesus Christ rules and reigns in majesty on earth for the actual "one thousand years." And what a celebration that future Feast of Tabernacles will be, with all the nations on the face of the earth represented in Jerusalem. And woe be to the nation that will refuse to show up for that celebration (Zech. 14:17–19)! Can any of us imagine how spectacular that celebration will be? One feature of the Feast of Tabernacles is the escalation of rejoicing which, like a great crescendo, reaches its climax on the spectacular eighth day.

"In that day 'HOLINESS TO THE LORD' shall be engraved on the bells of the horses. The pots in the Lord's house shall be like bowls before the altar [giant in size]. Yes, every pot in Jerusalem and Judah shall be holiness to the LORD of Hosts. Everyone who sacrifices shall come and take them and cook in them. In that day there shall no longer be a Canaanite in the house of the LORD of hosts" (Zech. 14:20, 21).

Therefore, both *Passover* and *Tabernacles* had future prophetic aspects attached to them. We know as well that the Day of Trumpets and the great Day of Atonement will have very sober fulfillments in the future. In addition, when a Bible reader studies and sees the beauty and the detailed precision of Christ fulfilling the typology of the Passover lamb, selected on the 10th day of Nisan and sacrificed on the 14th day, not a "bone of Him broken" as demanded by the Law, and then resurrected at the precise time as the "Wave-sheaf Offering of Firstfruits" three days later, he can only stand in amazement at the precision and glory of the outworking of God's divine time clock.

Furthermore, we now add to this evidence the fact that the Church of Jesus Christ came into existence at the precise time of the Feast of Pentecost. To say that the Church of Jesus Christ came into existence "on the Day of Pentecost" does not do justice to the specificity of what actually happened. The Day of Pentecost was a twenty-four hour day. The most important highlight, and the very focal point of that Day, was in the morning *hour* of the 50th day when the very special and very unique Offering of the Wave-loaves of bread was enacted. It was at that very cue that the Holy Spirit of

God took up His residence upon this earth, baptizing the disciples into one body, forming the Church of Jesus Christ (Acts 1:5 and 1 Cor. 12:13). The Hebrew-Christian scholar, Alfred Edersheim, in his book *The Temple, its Ministry and Services*, on page 266, 267, captures for us this phenomenon—

> For, as the worshippers were in the Temple, probably just as they were offering the wave-lamb and the wave-bread, the multitude heard that 'sound from heaven, as of a mighty rushing wind,' which drew them to the house where the apostles were gathered, there to hear 'everyone in his own language' 'the wonderful works of God.'

As I stated, the Hebrew prophets attached a prophetic significance to the Feast of Passover and to the Feast of Tabernacles. They said nothing prophetically about the Feast of Pentecost which dwells between these two Feasts. Obviously, the Feast of Pentecost is *parenthetical* in nature to the other two Feasts. And, so is the Church Age *parenthetical* between the Law Dispensation and the Kingdom Age. It is vitally important to recognize that the future prophetic significance of Pentecost is left to *the apostle Paul to unveil*. To Paul was specifically given the mystery of this Age of Grace (Eph. 3:1–13). It is therefore appropriate that the "mystery" concerning the Rapture of the Church would also be primarily revealed through Paul (Col. 1:24–27). We shall see in the remainder of this study that Paul was inspired to connect the resurrection of the saints of this age with the special Harvest Feast of Firstfruits, also called Pentecost.

Observations by Bible Teachers

Consequently, many Bible students in these last days have been and are interested in the prophetic aspects of these Feast days. Often they have focused upon the fall Feast of Israel and its related High Days. These celebrations and observances very well point to significant facts which will occur in the time of the events surrounding the Great Tribulation and the second coming of Jesus Christ.

J. N. Darby is often said to be the one most responsible for the school of Dispensational Bible teaching in the beginning of these last days. I do not believe for one second that John Nelson Darby invented the pretribulational Rapture doctrine, nor did he design dispensational Bible truth. He simply recognized these truths. If dispensational truth is found in the Scriptures, and it most certainly is, especially in the Scriptures of the apostle Paul, then we would have to assign the origin of the doctrine with Paul, no matter what blanks one may find about the subject in so-called "church history." J.N. Darby, himself, in the midst of a revival of premillennial prophetic teaching (in approx. 1830) reportedly attended a conference where there was a keen interest in studying the Feasts in Israel's calendar, as revealed by Moses in the Law. This was specifically for the purpose of considering their prophetic significance. It has been recently stated—

> Darby's *Synopsis* is replete with detailed, typological analysis of the Scriptures. He believed that just as Christ's atonement had been foreshadowed in the Levitical system (cf. Heb. 8:5; 10:1), so the restoration of Israel and the Rapture of the Church had been foreshadowed throughout the Old Testament. He maintained that there was 'peculiar grace', or blessing, for the Christian who understood the types, shadows and patterns found in the Scriptures.

See *For Zion's Sake* by Paul Richard Wilkerson, 2007, page 118. This book discusses in detail the role of John Nelson Darby in Christian Zionism.

Again, in very recent days many Bible teachers have reviewed the Feast Days more carefully in order to align biblical prophecies of the last days into some sequence. Some have done this very hastily, with a degree of erroneous presumption, usually leaving out the Rapture of the Church, or else assigning it to one of the fall "Appointed Times." I most earnestly pray that this Bible study will help clarify this aspect of the subject. You will note that I am going to very rigidly adhere to a literal following of Israel's liturgical calendar of the Feasts in this Bible study, which I think you will appreciate.

Most students of prophecy have recognized the Feast Days of Israel's calendar as being very important because the sufferings, death and resurrection of Jesus Christ were literally on schedule with various aspects of the Feast of Passover and the Offering of the Wave-sheaf of grain. And then, as I noted previously, the fact that the Church would be born on the very Day of Pentecost added further confirmation to the prophetic significance of the Feasts. This has caused most Bible students to take a careful look at all the Feast Days regarding their prophetic purposes. It appears that God has a revealed calendar by which He, in His sovereignty, is directing and scheduling all things. Thus, in the Mosaic Law this calendar is revealed and presented to the nation of Israel—and in the process of dispensational time it is being unfolded and fulfilled in an important historical sequence.

A standard work on the book of Leviticus (1899) was by S.H. Kellog. As to the prophetic nature of the Feast Days, he said, ". . . all who acknowledge the authority of the New Testament will recognize a yet more profound, and prophetic, spiritual meaning. Passover and Unleavened Bread not only looked backward, *but forward*." Kellog further stated that, like Passover, Pentecost was also "*prophetic*" (*Leviticus,* by Kellog, pgs. 458 and 460).

More recently, J. Vernon McGee, of international fame for his "*Through The Bible*" radio program, has stated, "These days of holy convocation served a twofold purpose; a practical purpose and a *prophetic purpose* . . . The primary purpose of these feast days was to give a prophetic picture of all future time. Each one of these feasts has found or will find a fulfillment in time . . . Each holy season had a particular and peculiar emphasis. The complete, prophetic dealings of God with this world in time are given here. Each feast was typical of some great event in the program of God for the world." McGee continued to say, "The typical meaning of Pentecost is not left to man's speculation . . . Pentecost is the birthday of the Church. It was fifty days after the resurrection of Christ that the Holy Spirit came. God was running according to His calendar and on time. They were to offer a new meal offering. That is a type of the Church. The Church is something new." (*Leviticus,* Vol. 2, pgs. 276-283).

Merrill F. Unger in his book, *The Baptism & Gifts of The Holy Spirit,* states on pages 155 and 156, "The Passover (Lev. 23:4–5), sacrificed on the fourteenth day of the first month, speaks of the death of Christ, and the feast of First-fruits (Lev. 23:9–14) on the morrow after the Sabbath three days later portrays the resurrection of Christ. Pentecost (Lev. 23:15–21) fifty days later sets forth the coming of the Holy Spirit (Acts 2:1–4) . . . The ancient Hebrew feast of Weeks (Lev. 23:15–21), as a type of what happened in Acts 2 . . . a new meal offering was to be presented to the Lord." Then Unger went into more detail about the typology of that sacrifice as it relates to the Church which is Christ's body.

We can see, therefore, by these few examples that an examination of certain prophetic aspects of these Feasts should not be some hasty speculation. Rather, it should be a wise and spiritual necessity, done with prayerful caution, asking for the illumination of the Holy Spirit, Who alone can "*Open my eyes, that I may behold wondrous things from Your Law.*" (Psalm 119:18).

Chapter Three

IS THE CHURCH TYPIFIED IN THE HEBREW SCRIPTURES?

Objection

Actually, biblical typology is a vital part of the divine record. In fact, typology is a very crucial and important factor in biblical doctrine. The book of Hebrews, which takes the Jewish believer out from under the Mosaic Law system into "better things," is literally filled with typologies from one end to the other. The same is true of the letter to the Galatians, which was written to prevent the Gentile believers from having the Law imposed upon them. Many times God illustrated things to come by the very events in the lives of the saints of old. Many theologians and Bible teachers recognize the field of "typology" as a very important part of biblical theology. Typologies must be studied with carefulness and caution because novices can enter that field with wild imaginations and attempt to prove almost anything. Any typology seen must be in strict compliance with sound biblical teaching. Therefore, the study of biblical typology is almost considered a scriptural science which demands concrete safeguards. Many prophecies of Christ were in the form of typologies. Sometimes the typologies are more vivid than certain direct prophecies.

Certain ones have objected to the idea of the Church being typified in the Hebrew Scriptures. They have argued that since the

Church was said to be a "mystery" not revealed in past ages (Eph. 3:1–6), therefore we will not see any types of the Church in the Old Testament, and certainly not in any of the Feast Days. It is true, of course, that there are no direct prophecies of the Church which is Christ's body revealed in the Hebrew Scriptures. Consequently, this is a legitimate concern and seems at first to be logical. If the Church was not specifically and directly prophesied in the Hebrew Scriptures, then it is also natural to ask how there could be any types of it.

The Hebrew prophets did see and know of the coming of their Messiah and the future events which concern their nation, especially the Kingdom, in the last days. These are the things which they prophesied in great detail, but they did not prophesy about the Church. However, we should be cautious to not quickly mandate from this that it automatically follows that there are no *types* of the Church in the Hebrew Scriptures. It is a fact that many of the types of Christ, Himself, were not known and realized by the Jewish believers until Christ revealed these to them. We read of the account in Luke where, after the resurrection of Christ, two disciples on the road to Emmaus met and listened to Christ, though they did not recognize Him. The text says, "And beginning with Moses and with all the prophets, He explained to them the things concerning Himself in all the Scriptures." And their response was, "Did not our hearts burn within us while He was speaking to us on the road, while He was explaining the Scriptures to us?" They obviously saw and heard things that they had never realized were in the Hebrew Scriptures.

Now the same may very well be true concerning the Church. If, indeed, we come to find, after the revelation of the Church, primarily through the apostle Paul, that the Holy Spirit opens our eyes to behold spiritual realities about the Church hidden in the Hebrew Scriptures—and there most surely are such to be found—then we should have explanations of these facts.

It is true that the Church (and the Church Age) was a mystery not revealed in past ages (Eph. 3:4, 5; Col. 1:24–27 and Rom. 16:25, 26). That is what these passages from Paul's epistles specifically say. However, it does not automatically follow that there were no *types* of the Church hidden in the Hebrew Scriptures. We do know that the Church and the Church Age were all known by God even before the foundation of the world (Eph. 1:4; 2 Tim. 1:9; Titus 1:2 and Acts 15:18 as examples). Therefore, I believe that when the mystery of the Church was revealed in the Greek Scriptures, then another phenomenon occurred. The Holy Spirit "lifted the veil," as it were, and many things began to appear in the Hebrew Scriptures which certainly no one at the time of the writing of these Scriptures understood, things concerning the Church of Jesus Christ.

In other words, the types and shadows about this age were themselves a "hidden mystery," remaining secret in the Hebrew Scriptures. These remained hidden until the Church was revealed. Then, under the illumination of the Holy Spirit guiding the authors of the New Testament, we can thereby look back into those ancient Scriptures and indeed behold beautiful pictures which God secreted into the pens of the Hebrew writers. These types lay dormant until the revelation about the Church was given. Thus, to say that there are certain types of the Church to be found in the Hebrew Scriptures does not actually contradict the fact of the Church and the Church Age being a mystery which was hidden in past ages; the typologies, themselves, were "hidden mysteries."

Positive Answers

The fact is, there were many things stated in the Hebrew Scriptures which were typical of and applicable to certain aspects of the Church, though those living in Old Testament times did not recognize them as such. In other words, these types were also a secret not understood by anyone until the later revelations given to Paul and the other apostles. Notice, please, that we have the following types and figures given to us from the writers of the Greek Scriptures themselves which will serve as examples:

1. In **Ephesians 5:22–33** the apostle Paul gave very beautiful exhortations to Christian husbands and wives in the Church of our Lord Jesus Christ. The Christian husband and wife are to pattern their relationship together after that example of Christ and the Church (verses 22–27). Two highlights of this

1. Adam was put into a deep sleep. This was not an ordinary sleep because God was actually going to perform an operation upon Adam.
2. God opened Adam's side and took a rib from his side.
3. God then closed up the wound in the side of Adam.
4. From this very substance God formed the woman.
5. This means the woman will be of the same substance as the man.
6. This means as well that the woman is vitally connected to the man.
7. Then, when Adam was awakened, God brought the woman, whom He had made, to him. What an amazing meeting that must have been!

This story is not a myth. It really happened! and antitypically, it is still happening to this very day! Yes, just as supernaturally as it happened at the beginning of time, so it is still happening at this very moment! Yes, every time a repentant sinner turns by faith to Christ's shed blood on his behalf, he will be created anew in the image of the Son. As I said before, Adam is specifically said to be a "type" of Christ (Rom. 5:14). Again, Jesus Christ is said to be *"the last Adam"* (1 Cor. 15:45). Now we are to realize that—

1. God placed His own Son, "the last Adam," into "a deep sleep"—*the very sleep of death itself.* Christ spoke of death as "sleep."
2. From Christ's spear-riven side came the substance, *the gospel of the grace of God*, the very shedding of the blood of Christ for our sins.
3. Christ's deadly wound was sealed by virtue of God's satisfaction with the substitutionary death of His Son. Christ would be *"raised up."*
4. From this very substance, which is the heart of the gospel of salvation, God supernaturally created and "formed the woman," the Church.

5. The woman thus became *"the Church which is Christ's body."* We are members of His very body, *"of His flesh and of His bones"* (Gen 2:23 and Eph.5:30).
6. Those who are "joined to the Lord [by faith] become *one spirit with Him"* (1 Cor. 6:17). Collectively, all believers form His present spiritual bride (Eph. 5:25–32). Thus the Church is formed as the vital members of Christ's very body.
7. And then, in perfect and glorious finality, this woman—that is, the Church—will be ultimately presented to Christ (Eph. 5:27) just as Eve was presented to Adam. What a meeting that is going to be!

In 2 Corinthians 11:2 this glorious event is spoken of by the apostle Paul as if he were the one, as Christ's ambassador, to "present" the bride to the Son. "For I have betrothed you to one husband that I may *present* you as a chaste virgin to Christ." And in the very next verse (11:3) Paul exhorted that, like *"Eve,"* our "minds should not be corrupted from the simplicity which is in Christ."

Now, should anyone want to deny that the Holy Spirit initially inspired Paul to tell us that this beautiful event which took place in the Garden of Eden was a type for the Church today? And, indeed, does anyone want to deny that all the beautiful truths which are included in this passage as it regards "Christ and the Church," both the ***type*** and the ***antitype***, *"are a great mystery"*? Herein, we have the clear example of one "mystery," that of the Church which is Christ's body, being prefigured by another "mystery," that of the creation of Eve.

In his book, *Basic Bible Interpretation*, by Chariot Victor Publishing (1991), Roy B. Zuck, who was the Chairman of the Department and Professor of Bible Exposition at the Dallas Theological Seminary, wrote concerning the qualifications for a scriptural typology on page 175 thusly—

> In summary, a type must have at least these five elements: [1] a notable resemblance or correspondence between the type and the antitype, [2] historical reality in both the type and antitype, [3] a prefiguring

or predictive foreshadowing of the antitype by the type, [4] a heightening in which the antitype is greater than the type, [5] and divine design.

Obviously, all five of these elements are perfectly and beautifully satisfied in this type which we have investigated. In addition, I would add another important "element" which I will call [6], that the text of Genesis 2:23 and 24 was specifically quoted by Paul. In addition, [7] Paul had already identified Adam as a "type" of Christ (Rom. 5:12–21, 1 Cor. 15:21, 45–49).

Could anyone, therefore, give a clearer and more satisfying explanation to the unbelieving Jew, who has placed his full trust in the veracity of the Hebrew Scriptures, of the reality of what God is doing in *true* Christianity today? And furthermore, to point out to that Jew the fact that God is performing this present supernatural creation *exactly on schedule,* just as He did with Eve during her creation on the "sixth day?" So it is that God is creating the Church on the *"sixth day"* of dispensational time! (Every dispensationalist should know what I mean by this last statement, for the present Age of Grace is the sixth dispensation on God's time clock, and the Kingdom Age is shortly to follow.)

2. In **Galatians 3:5–9** the apostle Paul points out Abraham as the standard of how we are saved—

> Therefore He Who supplies the Spirit to you and works miracles among you, does He do it by the works of the Law, or by the hearing of faith?—just as Abraham 'believed God, and it was accounted to him for righteousness' [Gen. 15:6]. Therefore know that only those who are of faith are sons of Abraham. And the Scripture, *foreseeing* that God *would justify the Gentiles by faith*, preached the gospel to Abraham beforehand, saying, 'In you all nations shall be blessed' [Gen. 12:3]. So then those who are of faith are blessed with believing Abraham. (Italics mine, J. L.)

Surely, no one would want to argue that this is not applicable to this present age of Gentile salvation which was *"foreseen"* in the Hebrew Scriptures.

3. In **Galatians 4:21-31** the apostle Paul furthermore said that Isaac, the son of Abraham, was an *"allegory"* (verse 24) portraying believers today in this Age of Grace. Without quoting the whole passage, I will simply itemize certain parts in the allegory. Paul stated the fact that Abraham had two sons and then contrasted the sonship of these two sons. Believers in this Age of Grace are represented by Isaac. Israelites under the Law are typified by Ishmael. One son (Ishmael) was from a "bondwoman"; whereas the other (Isaac) was from a "freewoman." One (Ishmael) was born "according to the flesh"; whereas the other (Isaac) was "through promise." Ishmael represents the Law Covenant from "Sinai which brings into bondage"; whereas Isaac represents "the promise" of salvation by faith in the principle of the Abrahamic Covenant. The one (Ishmael) represents earthly "Jerusalem in bondage"; whereas the other (Isaac) represents the "heavenly Jerusalem which is free, which is the mother of us all." Paul highlighted this "allegory" with the words, "Now we, brethren, *as Isaac was, are children of promise"* (verse 28).

Then Paul continued the "allegory" with the additional parallel fact—"But, as he who was born according to the flesh [Ishmael] then persecuted him [Isaac] who was born according to the Spirit, *even so it is now."*

That there is such an "allegory" concerning clear dispensational distinctions applicable to believers today from the Hebrew Scriptures was specifically stated!

4. **Genesis chapters 22, 23, 24 and 25**. All Bible teachers readily admit that the offering up of Isaac by his father, Abraham, in Genesis 22 is one of the boldest typologies in startling clarity in the Hebrew Scriptures. Isaac is primarily a type of Jesus Christ, as the well-beloved Son of His Father,

Who was offered in supreme sacrifice. The apostle Paul added to the story by stating that Abraham "concluded that God was able to raise him [Isaac] up, even from the dead, from which he received him in a figurative [or, a typical] sense" (Heb. 11:19).

And yet another aspect of this very story is its continuing unfolding in the drama of what happened after the typology of Isaac's being offered up as a sacrifice and his resurrection from the dead. There next emerged a much larger picture of what God has designed to do in broad dispensational time. We can look back in the book of Genesis to the story of Abraham obtaining a bride for his son, Isaac, and see a remarkable parallel with what God the Father is doing in this Church Age in obtaining a bride for His Son. The whole setting of that story will spell out not only this dispensation of time, but its relationship to the ages on either side of it.

Briefly given, in Genesis 22 Isaac was taken up on the hill to be a sacrifice. I say again, this is an incredibly clear picture of the death of God's Son, Jesus Christ. Isaac was received back as though he had risen from the dead (Hebrews 11:19). And then, in the very next chapter of Genesis (23), Abraham's wife, Sarah, died as a picture of Israel being set aside after the death of Messiah. In chapter 24 Abraham now sought to find a bride for Isaac, who had typically been sacrificed and resurrected from the dead. Isaac was very saddened by the death of his mother. Isaac would be "comforted" after the death of his mother (Gen. 24:67) by having a bride of his own.

What an amazing story about this bride! Abraham, the father of Isaac, *like God the Father of our Lord Jesus Christ*, sought a bride for his son. A messenger, the servant of Abraham, *much like a gospel preacher*, was sent into a far country, *as preachers today are sent into all the world*, being led by a holy angel, *representing the Holy Spirit* guiding the messengers today. He met a woman at the well, *illustrating a person's thirst for real life* (as in John 4:15). The messenger gave the *good news* to the woman at the well, and showed her the jewelry depicting *the riches of the many promises of God*. She heard that this one of whom he spoke is the heir, *much like Jesus Christ*, to all his father's wealth. She heard that he remained waiting to receive her if she would accept the invitation, *as is also true of Jesus Christ*. Though she had never seen the bridegroom, nor had she ever heard his voice, and though she could not touch him, and though to many this would sound as an idle tale—yet she believed, and said "Yes, I will go!" (Gen. 24:58). Hallelujah! This same situation is precisely stated of believers today through the words of Peter—"*And though you have not seen Him*, you love Him, *and though you do not see Him now*, but believe in Him, you greatly rejoice with joy inexpressible and full of glory, obtaining the outcome of your faith—the salvation of your souls" (1 Pet. 1:8 and 9). She is from the family of those who are *uncircumcised* and also represents a *vast multitude* (Gen. 24:60). She left her own family and traveled the long distance to ultimately meet the one she had accepted. And then finally, *at the close of a day*, she saw *him coming out to meet her* (verses 63–65)!

Chapter 24 is, therefore, completed. Now chapter 25 of Genesis takes up once again the story of Abraham, who received another wife and had many children by her—representing the revival of national Israel. And so we naturally once again ask the question, could some uninspired human author write out the story of this dispensational sequence any clearer—some 2000 to 4000 years in advance?

Perhaps one of the most striking things of all about this story, as it relates to the dispensational setting, is a traditional observation made by certain Jewish sages who studied this passage very carefully and concluded that Isaac *disappeared from the scene* after he was potentially offered up. Here is how it was recently written in *The International Jerusalem Post* (November 21-27, 2008) by Rabbi Reskin—

> First of all, what happened to Isaac immediately after the *akeda* [Isaac being offered, J. L.]? **He disappears**! The Biblical text is very clear, if problematic: 'Abraham returned to his lads'—the two young men who had accompanied father and son to the mountain, but whom Abraham told to remain behind with the donkey while the father and son went to worship God (Gen. 22:3, 5), And they rose up and went

together to Beersheba' (Gen. 22:19). Targum Yonatan reports that Isaac was **miraculously transported** to the Yeshiva [religious school, J. L.] of Shem and Eber, but the text does not tell us this. **The next time we meet Isaac (is) when Eliezer is returning from Aram Naharayim with Rebekah, his intended bride**—we are told: 'Isaac was just coming from Beer-lahai-roi, and was dwelling in the land of the Negev, and Isaac went out to commune [with God] in fields . . . and behold, the camels [of Eliezer and Rebekah] were coming.' (Only the bold is mine, J.L.)

Now this is an amazing tradition in Judaism. It is certainly a fact, which these Jews observed, that Isaac was not mentioned again until his meeting with his new bride. And, no, it is not stated in the Bible that he was "transported." And yet, such a tradition in the hearts of these Jewish sages also manifests a divine truth, that the antitypical Isaac (Jesus Christ), after His death and resurrection did, indeed, disappear from earth (as far as the lost world was concerned) and He was "miraculously transported" into heaven. And most certainly, the next time He will be seen in the drama of world events will be semi-privately—at the Rapture—when He comes to meet "His intended bride."

5. **Joseph, Moses and David**. Three men who stand as the very prominent types of the Messiah—who are recognized as such by both Jewish and Christian teachers alike— are Joseph, Moses and David. Jewish rabbis refer to the Messiah as either "Messiah ben Joseph" or "Messiah ben David" because of their own traditional recognition that these men prefigure the Messiah Who was to come. Both Joseph and David reigned over the people of Israel and served as obvious likenesses to Messiah. Moses is well understood as a picture of Messiah, not only because he came to rule over the nation of Israel, but also because of the clear passage in Deuteronomy 18:15–19 saying that another prophet

like Moses would arise and the nation of Israel would be accountable to Him.

It is interesting that in Stephen's message before the Sanhedrin, when he was about to be killed for his testimony, he reminded his audience of these three men—Joseph (Acts 7:9–15), Moses (Acts 9:20–44) and briefly, David (Acts 9:45, 46).

The first unique thing about all three of these men—and Stephen stresses this with the first two, Joseph and Moses—is that their appearance to Israel was in *two clearly distinct stages* separated *by a period of rejection*. During the first stage, in which each of them presented himself to Israel, he was rejected and *set aside into obscurity*. In Joseph's case "his brothers said to him, 'shall you indeed reign over us?'" (Gen. 37:8). In the case of Moses, his brethren said to him, "Who made you a prince and a judge over us?" (Exo. 2:14). In David's case, King Saul, who was Israel's carnal choice of a king, because of jealousy would prevent David from having the throne (1 Sam.18:8). With Joseph, the rejection was for some 20 years; in Moses' case it lasted for 40 years; and in David's situation it was for about 10 years. In the second stage, each of these men appeared in strength and great power and ruled over the nation of Israel.

The second unique thing about each of these men was their relationship to the Gentiles. Both Joseph and Moses actually took *Gentile brides* in their period of isolation. David, in his exile, was protected by Gentile people (1 Sam. 21:10; 22:3; 27:1) and literally aligned himself *to Israel's enemies from among the Gentiles*.

All these facts very clearly exhibit what will happen in the case of the Messiah, Himself. Today, like Joseph in the nation of Egypt, Christ is highly regarded among the Gentiles . And, like both Joseph and Moses, He is, in fact, calling out a Gentile bride.

6. Ruth the Gentile. The one book which contains very specific dispensational implications regarding the acceptance of the Gentiles is the story contained in the book of Ruth. Nor is it a mere coincidence that the Jewish people today are customarily encouraged to read the book of Ruth in their celebration of Shavuot (sometimes called *Hag Habikurim*, "The

Festival of Firstfruits,") or better known to us as *Pentecost*. Not only does the setting for this story emerge out of the backdrop of a very sad and bitter tragedy, but the account unfolds into a most tender and beautiful love story that takes place during the barley and wheat harvest time in Israel. This is why it is usually read and studied at the time of the Feast of Firstfruits (Pentecost). It perfectly coincides, not merely with the timing of the Feast, but, most importantly, with the prophetic substance of the story of Ruth. Reading the inspired book of Ruth is like dipping your hands into a small treasure chest of the most precious jewels. A surprising number of volumes have been written about the many reflections of light, as from sparkling diamonds of truth, which are to be found in this book.

The story has been called *"The Romance of Redemption."* There is a clear dispensational application to our own present age of Gentile salvation by this inspired story. A unique feature of this account is that this Gentile woman came to find *"grace"* in the eyes of a wealthy Jewish man (Ruth 2:2 and 10). Of course, this particular age is called "the Dispensation of the Grace of God" (see John 1:17; Acts 20:24; Rom. 5:2 and Eph. 3:2). The apostle Paul was inspired to say, *"through their* [the Jews'] *fall...salvation has come to the Gentiles"* (Rom. 11:11). This is exactly what happened in the book of Ruth. In addition, it has been noted by certain Jewish writers that the sad experience of Elimelech and his family of Jews who left the promised land much resembles the present state of the Jews in the Diaspora. Quoting from Shlomo Reskin once again (*The Jerusalem Post International*, "The Joy of Anticipation," June 6, 2003) we have these words,

> Elimelech . . . leaves the house of bread [Bethlehem] . . . ends up encountering a 'world of death and illusion.' The tale of Elimelech can be seen as a description of what happens to a Jewish family *in the Diaspora*. . . . Only when every Jew-by-birth recaptures the excitement, anticipation and preparation

of the Jew-by-choice will the true Messiah bring redemption to the world.

This story climaxes in the *midnight hour of secrecy* when a most unlikely heroine, an accursed Gentile (typical of the Gentiles of this age), who had found grace in the eyes of a mighty Jew of wealth (typical of Jesus Christ), places herself at his feet to claim the right of kinsman redemption (typical of the guarantee of Gentile blessing in the Abrahamic Covenent, Gen. 12:3 and Gal. 3:8). This virtuous woman was accepted because of his love for her. In turn, the precious fruit of their marriage becomes *"A Restorer of Life"* to Israel (Ruth 4:15 and Rom. 11:31).

Hebrew scholars tell us that the phrase, "[God] *Who did not withhold His kindness*," is found in only two places in the Hebrew Scriptures—**the story of Isaac and Rebecca** (Genesis 24:27), and **the story of Ruth and Boaz** (Ruth 2:20). Both these stories, I believe, were designed by God to prefigure this present Age of Grace. All praise, honor and glory be to God the Father and to His Son, Jesus Christ our Lord!

7. Of course, it is the purpose of this whole biblical study to demonstrate that the **Feast of Firstfruits, called Pentecost**, is a vivid example of the typology in the Hebrew Scriptures which prefigures, in different ways, the Church of Jesus Christ today. Consequently, I will allow the remainder of this study to speak for itself. Briefly stated, the Holy Spirit inspired James to write and make a general reference to the Church of Jesus Christ as being "brought forth by the Word of truth so that we might be, as it were, the *firstfruits* among His creatures" (James 1:18).

8. **Enoch**. I am going to save a separate chapter in this book for this very unusual and even "mysterious" person named Enoch. Though only a few verses are originally written about him in Genesis, yet an amazing amount of very interesting tradition has arisen concerning him.

More Examples

For many more references in the Greek Scriptures where applications from the Hebrew Scriptures were made for this present age, see the following examples:

Acts 4:11; Eph. 2:20 and 1 Pet. 2:7 ". . . which has become the chief cornerstone." This is from Psalm 118:22. It is applied to Christ in His present position.

1 Pet. 2:6 "Behold, I lay in Zion a chief cornerstone, elect, precious, . . ." Again, this is applied to Christ's present position. From Isaiah 28:16.

1 Pet. 2:8 "A stone of stumbling and a rock of offense." The same as above. Taken from Isaiah 8:14.

Acts 13:46 and 47 Paul said concerning Christ's instruction as to their ministry, ". . . behold, we turn to the Gentiles. For so the Lord has commanded us: 'I have set You [Messiah] as a light to the *Gentiles*, that You should be for salvation to the ends of the earth.'" Taken from Isaiah 49:6.

Rom. 10:19 "But I say, did not Israel know? First Moses says: 'I will provoke you to jealousy by *those who are not a nation, I will move you to anger by a foolish nation.*'" Taken from Deuteronomy 32:21.

Rom. 10:20 "But Isaiah is very bold and says: 'I was found by *those* [the Gentiles] who did not seek Me: I was made manifest to those who did not ask for Me.'" Taken from Isaiah 65:1.

Acts 26:22, 23 Paul makes a declaration of his ministry in these words ". . . saying no other things than those which the prophets and Moses said would come—that the Christ would suffer, that He would be the first to rise from the dead, and would proclaim light to the Jewish people and to the *Gentiles*." Taken from Isaiah 42:6 and 7.

Rom. 15:9 ". . . and that the Gentiles might glorify God for His mercy, as it is written: 'For this reason I will confess to You among the *Gentiles*, and sing to Your name.'" From 2 Samuel 22:50.

Rom. 15:10 "And again He says: 'Rejoice, O *Gentiles*, with His people!'" From Deuteronomy 32:43.

Rom. 15:11 "And again: 'Praise the LORD, all you *Gentiles*! Laud Him, all you peoples!'" From Psalm 117:1.

Rom. 15:12 "And again, Isaiah says: 'There shall be a root of Jesse; and He Who shall rise to reign over the **Gentiles**, in Him the *Gentiles* shall hope.'" From Isaiah 11:10.

Rom. 15:21 ". . . but as it is written: 'To whom He was not announced, they shall see; and those who have not heard shall understand.'" From Isaiah 42:15.

It is evident from all these references that there should be no question about the fact that, in several different ways, characteristics of this age were typified, allegorized, and numerous applications were made concerning them from the Hebrew Scriptures. Of course, this is not to say that the very unique aspect of the Church—of making "one New Man" (literally, a new species) from both *Jewish believers* and *Gentile believers*, baptizing them into one body—was thus fully revealed. However, to say that the Church, because it was said to be a "mystery," is therefore never typified in the Old Testament is an overreaction to the "mystery" aspect of the Church and the Church Age. The facts are well established that some aspects of the Church were typified in different ways in the Hebrew Scriptures. That there would come an age of God's nearness to the Gentile people is now clearly understood. However, these specific typologies *were not known or understood* until they came to light through the revelations given to Paul and the other writers of the Greek Scriptures. In other words, like the Church itself, the types were a "mystery" as well. They had to remain dormant in the Hebrew Scriptures until the time came when God wanted them revealed. In saying all this, I am showing that we should not be fearful of recognizing that there can be a picture of the Church of Jesus Christ in the Feast of Pentecost if the Scriptures so testify.

Chapter Four

IMPORTANT CLARIFICATIONS ABOUT THE FEASTS OF ISRAEL

How Many Feasts Are There?

One foremost clarification should be made about the Feasts which God gave to Israel. Many Christian preachers and writers, in telling about the prophetic nature of the Feasts, will characteristically say that there were "seven Feasts" given to Israel by Moses. Technically speaking, this is not at all accurate! Unfortunately, many versions of the Bible will translate two different Hebrew words as "feast." The first and actual Hebrew word for feast is *hag, chag* or *haggim* (plural). *Hag,* or some would say *chag,* simply means "to move in a circle" or "to dance," which demonstrates the nature of a feast or festival. This word is used of only three specific events on Israel's calendar. These three Feasts were: (1) the Feast of Unleavened bread, (2) the Feast of Weeks (Pentecost), and (3) the Feast of Tabernacles. In fact, the Law very clearly indicates that there were only *"three Feasts"* for the nation of Israel (Exo. 23:14–17; 34:18, 22, 23; Deut. 16:16 and 2 Chron. 8:13).

A second Hebrew word is used which is *mowed, moed* or *mo'adim* (plural) and this has the specific meaning of "appointed time or season." There are indeed seven *mo'adim* in the liturgical calendar as revealed by God through Moses. The *mo'adim* ("appointed times") were composed of certain Holy Days and special Offerings.

But only three of these *mo'adim* are also qualified as *haggim* or Feasts. It was only on these three *haggim* that all the males were required to appear before the Lord in Jerusalem. These three Feasts are thus popularly known as the "Three Pilgrimage Festivals." The problem has been that many Bible translations and teachers have referred to all these seven *mo'adim* as "the Feasts of Israel," whereas, in reality, only three of these appointed times (*mo'adim*) were Feasts (*haggim*). S. H. Kellogg, in his standard work on *The Book of Leviticus*, explains this distinction on pages 447 and 448.

Several Bible translations make this important distinction. One is *The Holy Scriptures, A New Translation*, by the Jewish Publication society of America, in both their 1917 version and the 1962 version; this translation is also the basis for the *Pentateuch & Haftorahs* which is read by the Jewish people in the whole English speaking world. *The Emphasized Bible*, by Rotherham and the *New American Standard Bible* also make this important distinction.

Also, remember that this calendar of events is not the same as Israel's Civil Calendar which came much later in the history of the nation and had additional national days of special observance. The calendar which was revealed through Moses has sometimes been referred to as the "Liturgical Calendar" because it has to do primarily with the religious rites and celebrations throughout its year. All these "Appointed Times" and special "Offerings," as revealed by Moses, can be enumerated in the following manner under seven or eight sections (see Leviticus 23), but remember, only three of these sections are to be properly understood as Feasts.

There are eight *mo'adim* if we count the regular Sabbath day which is first listed. The first of the *mo'adim* according to Leviticus 23 was the regular seventh day Sabbath which continued throughout the year. In addition, there were *seven* "appointed times of the LORD" of a special nature and scattered in a particular pattern throughout the year—

No. 1.

The first "Appointed Time" is on the afternoon hours of the 14th day of the first month (Abib, later called Nisan). This was the special ***sacrifice of the Passover lambs*** (Lev. 23:5). This is done on "the evening of the fourteenth day." The lambs would then be roasted and prepared for dinner which was to be eaten after sunset, beginning the fifteenth day. This fourteenth day is actually called *"the Preparation Day"* for the Feast which begins with the Passover supper just after the conclusion of that day (see 2 Chron. 35:6, 10 and 16; John. 19:31, 42 and Luke 23:54). Remember that each day on the Jewish calendar begins with the setting of the sun and is marked from sunset to sunset. Thus, just after the sunset *closing* this 14th day, the fifteenth day begins with the Jewish people sitting down and eating their Passover Suppers.

No. 2. (and the 1st Feast)

The second "Appointed Time" and the first "Feast" was on the 15th day through the 21st day of the same month. This was called the *"**Feast of Unleavened Bread**"* (Lev. 23:6–8). The first day of this Feast began in the evening with the eating of the Passover Supper. This first day was also regarded as a special "High Sabbath" day. In later years this whole Feast of seven days was also commonly called *"Passover"* (Hebrew, *Pesah*) — See Luke 22:1 and Acts 12:3, 4. This Feast had two special High Sabbaths, one on the 15th day and one on the 21st day.

No. 3.

The third "Appointed Time" took place during the Feast of Unleavened Bread (or Passover), on the morning after a regular Sabbath which would occur during this week. On the morning of the first day of the week during this Feast the special **Wave-sheaf Offering** of the *"Firstfruit"* sample of spring harvest grain was to take place. This was not a separate Feast, nor should it ever be called or designated as "the Feast of Firstfruits" as is sometimes erroneously done. It was only a very *special offering* of the early "Firstfruit" sample which occurs during the Feast of Unleavened Bread (Lev. 23:9–14). This special offering consisted of a small bundle of early grain, sometimes called "the Omer" in reference to the weight or amount of grain. It primarily served as a *sample* of the greater harvest to be celebrated some 50 days later. At the time of Christ this special offering was still performed on a Sunday morning, though in later Jewish tradition it began to be done on the morning after the first High Sabbath (the 15th) during the Feast of Unleavened Bread.

No. 4. (and the 2nd Feast)

The fourth "Appointed Time" and the second Feast is the **"Feast of Harvest of Firstfruits"** (Exo. 23:16; 34:22 and Lev. 23:17). This is also designated in the Scriptures as "the Feast of Firstfruits" (Exo. 23:16; 34:22 and Num. 28:26). Among the Jewish people it is most commonly called the *"Feast of Weeks"* (Hebrew, *Shavuot*, Exo. 34:22; Num. 28:26 and Deut. 16:10) because of the seven weeks which transpire from the offering of the "Wave-sheaf" at the Passover celebrations. In the book of Acts it is called by the Greek word, *"Pentecost"* (50th), because of its celebration on the 50th day (Acts 2:1). Upon counting seven weeks (49 days) after the "Wave-sheaf Offering" during the Feast of Unleavened Bread, on the 50th day came Pentecost. We will note later some of the other names given to this Feast. This was only a one day Feast. On this day was the special *"New Grain Offering"* in the form of two loaves of bread waved in the air similar to the waving of the *"Wave-sheaf Offering"* at Passover. This day was a special High Sabbath. (See Lev. 23:15–21.) This is the Feast day that we are going to focus upon during this Bible study.

No. 5.

The fifth "Appointed Time" took place on the first day of the seventh month. This is the day upon which the **"Blowing of Trumpets"** or horns (Hebrew, *Shofa*r) took place. This is not designated as a Feast day (*hag* or *chag*), but it is a special High Sabbath (Lev. 23:23–25). In later years (some say in Nehemiah's day) this would become the first day of the year on Israel's Civil Calendar.

No. 6.

The sixth "Appointed Time" was on the 10th day of the same month and was called "***The day of Atonement***" (Hebrew, *Yom Kippur*). On this day was the special offering of the "Scapegoat." This day was a very special High Sabbath, but not a Feast (*hag*) day (Lev. 23:26–32).

No. 7. *(and the 3rd Feast)*

The seventh "Appointed Time" and the third Feast was on the fifteenth day of the same month and began the "***Feast of Tabernacles***" (also called "*Booths,*" Hebrew, *Sukkat*). See Lev. 23:34–43. This Feast was celebrating the fall harvest and was therefore also called "*The Feast of Ingathering*" (Lev. 23:39) because at this time they had completed, or were completing, the final ingathering of the crops of the land. This Feast was said to be seven days long—however, the added eighth day was an important crescendo to the whole Feast and there was great rejoicing. This Feast had two High Sabbaths, one on the first day (15th), and one on the eighth day (22nd).

Here is a brief listing or summary of these seven "Appointed Times" (*mo'adim*)—

1. The Passover sacrifice, 1st Month, 14th Day.
2. Feast (*hag*) of Unleavened Bread, 1st Month, 15th—21st Day.
3. Wave-sheaf Offering of grain, the morning after the Sabbath during the Feast.
4. Feast (*hag*) of Firstfruits, on the morning after seven Sabbaths had passed from the Wave-sheaf Offering.
5. The Blowing of Trumpets, 7th Month, 1st Day of the Month.
6. The Day of Atonement, 7th Month, 10th Day of the Month.
7. Feast (*hag*) of Booths or Tabernacles, 7th Month, 15th Day—22nd Day.

The Important Arrangement of Pentecost

It is generally observed that all these "Appointed Times" are clustered into two groups. The first group was in the spring harvest season and the latter in the fall harvest season. Numbers 1, 2, 3 and 4 are in the first grouping and take place primarily in the spring in connection with the Feast of Unleavened Bread (Passover). Numbers 5, 6 and 7 take place in the fall season and are clustered at the time of the Feast of Tabernacles.

However, a more careful scrutiny will show that there were actually *three* groups. Number 4, the Feast of *Shavuot* (also called *Weeks* or *Pentecost*), though it is related to the earlier offering of the Wavesheaf at Passover seven weeks earlier, actually stands *alone by itself*. The reason Pentecost is to be viewed as standing alone by itself is because of several unusual facts or characteristics about this Feast which make it different from the others. These facts will now be brought out in the following manner—

1. The Feast is Parenthetical

First, Pentecost is merely a one day Festival which obviously falls between the Feast of Unleavened Bread (Passover) of seven days and the Feast of Tabernacles of eight days. Falling between the Feast of Passover and the Feast of Tabernacles allows Pentecost to be viewed as **parenthetical** in nature. This placement is very suggestive of dispensational truth. Everyone admits that if there is any Feast which typifies aspects of the Church, it would be Pentecost simply because that was "the Day" upon which the Church was born. In addition, it is the observation of most dispensational Bible teachers that the Church Age itself is **parenthetical** in nature to the two Ages on each side of it. Christ was born and ministered under the Law Dispensation. He offered to Israel the long anticipated Kingdom during His earthly ministry. However, there was a national rejection of Israel's own Messiah (Prince). Thus the anticipated Messianic Kingdom was "postponed" until a future date when the Messiah would return in great power and wrath to rule and reign here on earth, just as we saw in the examples of Joseph, Moses and

David. This "Mystery" Age, i.e., the present Church Age, was *parenthetical* in nature. It takes place in the intervening period of time between the first and second comings of Jesus Christ.

2. The "Mystery" Feast

In addition, from a Jewish perspective, this Feast has sometimes been looked upon as, and has even been called, a ***"mystery"*** festival (see *the Jerusalem Post, International Edition*, May 26-June 1, 2006, *"What's in a name?"* by Rabbi Reskin). The reason given for referring to this Feast as a *"mystery"* festival was first of all because "the name (of the Feast) does not define its essence." The name *Passover* has reference to the Passover lamb whose blood protected the firstborn of all the children of Israel. The name *Tabernacles* has reference to the dwelling places of the Israelites during their wilderness journey. The Feast of Weeks or Pentecost, on the other hand, only speaks of the *weeks or days* leading up to the celebration. This says "nothing whatsoever about the Feast" or its relationship to Israel. Of course, it is very interesting that the "Church which is Christ's body," born on the Day of Pentecost, was also said to be a "***mystery***" (Eph. 3:1–7).

3. Not Connected to any Historical Event of Israel

In addition, the "mystery" aspect of Shavuot (Pentecost), as explained by the Jerusalem Post article, is not merely because of the name, but primarily because it is **not connected** by Moses **to any historical event in Israel's early history** as are Passover and Tabernacles. Passover is in remembrance of Israel's deliverance out of Egypt. Tabernacles is in remembrance of Israel dwelling in tents or booths for 40 years in the wilderness. Pentecost, being *parenthetical* in nature in its actual biblical setting, is not connected to anything in Israel's historic journey as are the other two Feasts. Much later in Jewish history the Pharisaic tradition concerning this Feast day was to try and find some national connection for it. After observing that the time period between the first Passover and Israel's arrival at the foot of Mount Sinai was about 50 days, they connected

Pentecost with the giving of the Law from Sinai. They did this even though it is admitted by all that the Scriptures themselves never specifically make this connection. However, this association in "tradition" was only made in an effort to make some sense out of the Feast in relationship to Israel, other than simply being a spring harvest celebration. (The Feast could and was only to be observed once Israel had entered into the Promised Land.) We might say, concerning the Church of Jesus Christ, that it, as well, is not vitally connected to anything concerning Israel's historic beginning.

On the other hand, it is true that when the Rapture of the Church takes place, which I believe is typified by Pentecost, the Law of Moses will automatically be reinstituted into the lives and practice of Jews saved on earth during the final week of years including the Great Tribulation. In this respect, the tradition of Judaism, which celebrates the giving of the Law at Shavuot (Pentecost) some 50 days after Passover, is very interesting.

4. The 50 Days

This Feast of Pentecost was to be observed after a 50 day interval of time. Actually, the name *Pentecost* is simply the Greek word for 50. One might ask the question, "Why did God specify that they count off 50 days?" and "What is the significance of the number 50?" "Why not," we may ask, "did God not say '20 days' or '40 days'?" In a practical way, we might answer that the harvest may take 50 days to fully mature. Of course, in reality, a harvest reaping may vary in time from year to year, depending on the growth and the weather as to when it is actually reaped. The 50th day simply commemorated the reaping of the harvest and did not mark the actual harvest event. Consequently, the number 50 must have further important significance!

Later we will discuss in more detail the significance of the 50 days. Suffice it to say here, the number 50 in Scripture signifies **"*fullness* or *completion*"** for whatever purpose God has in mind. This was certainly true for celebrating the 50th year of release when God decreed that the people could return to their properties that may have been sold. Again, for instance, if it is the time period when

"God is calling out a people from among the Gentiles for His name" (Acts 15:14), then the number 50 would simply signify whatever actual time period it would take to arrive at the "completion" or "fullness" of that calling. Therefore, when the apostle Paul spoke of the time when "the *fullness* of the Gentiles shall come in" (Rom. 11:25), this would be like saying "the antitypical 50th day will have arrived." So it is a key factor which we shall note more fully as we move along in this study—that Pentecost essentially signifies that *"the time of fullness or completion has come,"* no matter how short or how long the actual time period will have lasted.

5. The Law was given After Fifty days

In a moment we will discuss in detail the modern Jewish custom of celebrating the giving of the Law at the Feast of Shavuot or Pentecost. However, as originally given by Moses, Shavuot had no connection with the giving of the Law. *The Encyclopedia Judaica* (1972 edition) says it was not until the second century of the Common Era that reference is made to Shavuot as having any historical connection to the giving of the Law (Vol. 14, page 1320). In other words, the Feast of Pentecost remains a harvest celebration in its original setting. Now it is true that in actual chronological calculations, the Law was given from Mount Sinai just over 50 days after the first Passover in Egypt (Exo. 19:1, 16). However, this fact may actually only have significance in typifying the **reinstitution of the Law** after the prophetic fulfillment of the Feast Day of Pentecost, i.e., after the Rapture of the Church.

6. The Reading of the Book of Ruth

As I explained earlier, it is the custom of the Jewish people to read the book of Ruth at the time of celebrating Shavuot (Pentecost). This is because the major story in the book of Ruth took place at the time of the spring harvesting in Israel. Her romance begins at the time of the first barley harvest (Ruth 1:22) and climaxes at the wheat harvest (2:23). Because of the obvious spiritual typology in the book of Ruth, it is very significant that the Jewish people themselves recognize its relationship with Shavuot. Pentecost carries with it the recognition of **Gentile acceptance and salvation**. This will be a highly important realization for the Jewish people at the time of the Rapture of the Church.

This custom among the Jews is an obvious carryover of the fact that *Shavuot* is indisputably related to the Firstfruit Harvest season and not to the Law. I say again, the whole setting of the book of Ruth takes place during the *Firstfruit Harvest season*. In addition, the story is a beautiful account of the "kinsman redemption" of a Gentile who came to embrace the God of Israel. This story is loaded with dispensational significance as it is reflective upon the subject before us of the Pentecostal Rapture of the Church. In this connection, the Feast of Pentecost or Weeks is related in a very beautiful and outstanding way to the theme of *GENTILE* redemption.

7. Under the Civil Calendar of the Jews
Pentecost is the Last Feast to be Observed in the Year

Interestingly enough, because of the arrangement of the later Jewish Civil New Year, beginning with *Rosh Hashanah* on the first day of Tishu and the blowing of the Shofar trumpets, Pentecost or Shavuot actually becomes the ***last and final festival of the civil year***. Sukkut (Tabernacles) and Pesah (Passover) are the first two Feasts in the order of the Civil Calendar and Pentecost thereby becomes the last. The Jews themselves take note of this—See *Celebrating The Jewish Holidays*, page 116, Crescent Books, New York. Because of Israel's national change in later years to function under a Civil Calendar, which begins on the first day of Tishu (Sept.-Oct.) instead of Abib or Nisan (March-April) of the Sacred Year Calendar, this very interesting arrangement has come about. In other words, if it is true that Pentecost signifies the Rapture of the Church, as I believe the apostle Paul says it does, then when the Rapture occurs, the very next thing on God's time clock begins a new time period in dealing with Israel in the last days.

8. Shavuot (Pentecost) is Missing in the Kingdom Celebration of the Feast

Herein is a very significant fact. In the prophecy of the book of Ezekiel, he spoke about the future Kingdom celebrations of the Feasts. However, he entirely leaves out mentioning any celebration for Shavuot. It is noticeably *absent* in Ezekiel 45:21–25. Only Passover and Tabernacles are mentioned, and the "parenthetical" Feast is absent. Is this not indicative of the fact that the ***divine purpose for Pentecost*** (i.e., the Rapture of the Church) ***has already been completed before the Kingdom is established***? It is only the preliminary purpose for Pentecost which had been fulfilled at the beginning of the Age of Grace.

9. The Short and Abrupt Nature of Pentecost

An additional observation which needs to be made is the obvious short and abrupt nature of Pentecost in comparison to the other two Feasts. The other two Feasts last for an extended period of time—seven days for the Feast of Unleavened Bread and eight days for the Feast of Tabernacles. In total contrast, the Feast of Pentecost bears the appearance of being unusually ***short and abrupt***—just like the Rapture of the Church.

10. The only Feast that does not have a Set Calendar Date

One final observation is the very interesting fact that the Feast of Pentecost is the only Feast on Israel's calendar which actually ***does not have a specified calendar date*** designated for its observance. The Feast of Unleavened Bread was designated to be observed on the 15th through the 21st days of the first month of Abib. The Feast of Tabernacles was designated for the 15th through the 22nd day of the seventh month (Tishri). Even The Passover sacrifice was designated for the 14th day of the first month. The Shofar was designated for the 1st day of the seventh month. The Day of Atonement was designated for the 10th day of the seventh month. The special Offering of the Wave-sheaf of Firstfruits was designated for the day after the Sabbath during the Feast of Unleavened Bread on the first month of Abib. However, there is neither *month* nor *date* specified for Pentecost in the divine revelation. Pentecost was only designated by its 50 day counting from the Offering of the Wave-sheaf. Because of this 50 day counting, it was understood that this Feast would obviously vary as to the calendar date from year to year. Please remember, it was only later Jewish tradition which assigned Shavuot to the 6th day of Sivan.

Now, as I stated in the Introduction to this study, Pentecost was the only Feast on Israel's liturgical calendar which, as it typified the Rapture, is not subject to the error of "date setting." This is demonstrated two ways: first, by the simple fact that there is no date or month specified in the Hebrew text for its observance; second, by the fact that the 50 days leading to it only symbolize "fullness or completion."

Relationship of Shavuot to the Law

Rabbi Reskin, who wrote the article referred to earlier about the "mystery" aspect of Shavuot, also explained that because of the unusual nature in the setting of this Feast, an important controversy arose between the Pharisees and Sadducees in the proximity of the New Testament period of time. Though the Feast obviously has an agricultural significance, yet in an attempt to associate it with Israel's historic beginnings, the Pharisees came to view it as pointing to the giving of the Law from Mount Sinai which was approximately fifty days after the Passover. However, it is admitted that "the Bible never identifies Shavuot (the Feast of Weeks) as the day of the revelation at Sinai" (*Shlomo Reskin, Jerusalem Post, International Edition,* June 6, 2003). The Sadducees said that Shavuot is "relating not at all to the Exodus, but only to the agricultural reality of the land of Israel . . . a thanksgiving for an agricultural rather than an historical reason" (2006 article, *Jerusalem Post*). Rabbi Reskin also points out in an earlier article that the giving of the Law actually *"followed"* the fiftieth day from the Passover in Egypt. (See also, *The Jerusalem Post, International Edition*, Shlomo Reskin, *"Something doesn't add up,"* May 21, 1999.) In this 1999 article Reskin states,

"Shavuot is merely an agricultural festival—the celebration of the first fruits—and biblically speaking, it only coincidentally works out to fall on *the day before* the Revelation (from Sinai)."

Nevertheless, the oral tradition of the Pharisees of connecting Shavuot to the Law came to prominence before the destruction of Jerusalem and the Temple in A.D. 70. This tradition of Shavuot commemorating the giving of the Law has remained ever since. In addition, a new name was even given to this Feast to seal this relationship—*Hag Matar Torahteinu*—which simply means "The Feast of the Giving of our Torah." Consequently, today, when the Jewish people celebrate Shavuot they do so with an emphasis upon commemorating the receiving of the Law from Sinai. However, the fact is that in the biblical record, Shavuot was not even practiced at the time of the giving of the Law (there were no grain fields in Sinai). In addition, in actual biblical chronology, the Law appears to have been given when, or just after, the fifty days had transpired.

For a more complete explanation and discussion of this issue, see my book, *The Threefold Order of the Resurrection of the Righteous*, chapter three, under "The Timing of the Offering."

It is also to be noted that the Sadducees were not the only group among the Jewish people who rejected the oral tradition of the Pharisees on this matter. The Karaite sect of Judaism still to this day carries on the timing of Shavuot to always occur on a Sunday.

This sect historically had its official beginning in about the eighth century. Nevertheless, they trace its doctrinal teachings to the first century, and some take the tradition all the way back to the time of the kings Rehoboam and Jeroboam, when the northern ten tribes split from the southern two tribes of Judah and Benjamin. The group is characterized by its primary denial of the Talmudic-Rabbinical traditions. (See *Encyclopedia Judaica*, Vol. 10, pages 761-785, 1972 edition.)

They referred to themselves as "People of the Scriptures." The one dictum that the leader (one named Anan) stated—"search thoroughly in the Torah and do not rely on my opinion." In addition, they placed no "restriction on individual understanding of the Scriptures." They reject the "oral law," that is, the traditional laws of rabbinic Judaism. Their emphasis is on "searching the Scriptures for right guidance." This would remind Christians of the Jews Paul met at Berea as recorded in Acts 17:10–14. It was stated of them that "they were more noble-minded than those of Thessalonica, for they received the word with great eagerness, examining the Scriptures daily, to see whether those things were so."

The Karaites held similar antitraditional beliefs as did the Sadducees of the time of Christ. As to the specific date for the celebration of Pentecost—"The Feast of Weeks [*Shavuot*] falls on the 50th day following the Saturday [Sabbath] of the Passover week [in accordance with the literal interpretation of Lev. 23:11, which the Talmud interprets in a different manner], and is therefore always on a Sunday." (*Encyclopedia Judaica*, 1972 edition, Vol. 10, page 779.)

Of course, it is indirectly the purpose of this study to show that immediately after the antitypical fulfillment of Pentecost in the Rapture of the Church, the Law will again be instituted. When one looks into the period called the Great Tribulation, as in Matthew 24, he will see the Law of Moses again being practiced. In Israel the Temple will have been *erected along with its services*, the animal sacrifices will be *reinstated,* and Sabbath *observance* will again be observed, etc., etc. (see as an example Matt. 24:15 and 20). All these facts place the Feast of Pentecost in a very special and unique perspective.

In Summary

In summary, concerning the particular arrangement of *Shavuot* (Feast of Weeks or Pentecost) as it fits into the calendar of events of "The Appointed Times of The Lord," I have made the following observations of significance:

1. Pentecost can be viewed as standing **parenthetical** in nature, falling in sequence between the Feast of Passover and the Feast of Tabernacles;
2. Pentecost has been referred to as a **"mystery"** festival, first because its name does not tell us anything about the nature of the Feast. Second, because—

3. Pentecost is ***not related to any event in Israel's original historic beginning*** as were Passover and Tabernacles.
4. Pentecost is identified merely by ***the time* (50 days)** until its celebration. This time is suggestive of the principle of "***fullness* or *completion***" for whatever purpose God has designed.
5. In the literal biblical chronology, as observed by certain Jewish scholars themselves, the giving of ***the Law*** from Sinai would more likely ***immediately follow*** the seven week time period and the celebration of *Shavuot* (Pentecost) on the fiftieth day.
6. The Feast becomes related to the time of ***Gentile salvation*** by the inspired record of the book of Ruth. Therein one, "without Christ," an "alien from the commonwealth of Israel," a "stranger from the covenants of promise," "having no hope" and "without God in the world" is "brought near" by the "grace" and love of a "kinsman redeemer" (Eph. 2:11–13 and Ruth 2:20).
7. Under the Civil Calendar of Israel, which is used today, Pentecost would be ***the final festival event before a new year*** begins for the nation.
8. Pentecost is ***left out*** in the mention of the Feasts for the Kingdom Age. This may indicate that its fulfillment has already taken place.
9. The ***short and abrupt*** nature of Pentecost, in comparison to the other two Feasts, is indicative of the nature of the Rapture of the Church of Jesus Christ.
10. The fact that there is ***no month or day of the month*** specified for its observance, as there was with all the other Feasts and Appointed Times, enhances the fact that what Pentecost ultimately typifies—i.e., the Rapture of the Church—is also dateless and only accomplished after the "fullness (50) of the Gentiles comes in" according to God's determination.

It should be observed that every one of the ten facts, which I just listed, points very clearly to the Feast of Pentecost as being prophetically applicable to many aspects of the present *Church Age*.

As stated earlier, none of these Feasts, Holy Days and special Offerings should be confused with the later Civil holidays which came after certain events in Israel's history. These other holidays are:

Purim (Lots), which originated in the days of Queen Esther; *Rosh Hashannah* (the Civil New Year), which was said to have originated in the days of Ezra-Nehemiah (Neh. 8:1–12); and *Hanukkah* (also called "Dedication" or "Lights"—John 10:22) which originated after the desecration of the Temple by the Greek king, Antiochus Epiphanes.

Chapter Five

PRELUDE TO PENTECOST

Offering of the Wave-sheaf of Firstfruits

As I have previously stated, at the time of Christ under the rule of the Sadducees, the ritual Offering of the Firstfruits of grain took place on the *day after* the regular 7th day Sabbath which fell during the Feast of Unleavened Bread or Passover. That meant this Offering would always occur on a Sunday morning. However, before the destruction of Jerusalem in A.D. 70, and in accordance with Pharisaic traditions which had taken over the high priest leadership in Israel, the Offering of the Firstfruits came to be celebrated on the day after the High Sabbath of Nisan 15, and not after the regular 7th day Sabbath which occurred during the Passover celebrations. Thereafter the Offering only rarely took place on a Sunday morning. Consequently, Shavout ("Weeks" or Pentecost), which comes seven weeks or 50 days later, as celebrated in Judaism according to this timing today, also rarely occurs on a Sunday.

Now, this first special Offering of the Wave-sheaf consisted of a sampling or a handful of the early grain, either as a Sheaf (bundle) of freshly cut grain or as an Omer (measure—Exo.16:36) of threshed grain. Therefore it is also sometimes called "The Offering of the Omer." This Offering was uniquely waved up in the air "before the Lord," as if it were to be directly received by God in heaven. Since it was for the Lord, after the waving only a designated priest would be allowed to take it for his own use.

I have previously discussed in my book, *The Day Christ Died as Our Passover,* how this Offering was a beautiful type of Christ's bodily resurrection and ascension up to the Father. In addition, it stands as the guaranteed basis of the future resurrection of the saints. This is stated twice in 1 Corinthians 15:20 and 23 —

> But now Christ is risen from the dead, and has become the Firstfruits *of those who have fallen asleep.* . . . But each in his own order [to be resurrected]: Christ the Firstfruits, *afterward those who are Christ's at His coming.*

So it is that this Offering served as a token blessing of the greater spring Harvest of Firstfruits to be celebrated fifty days later. As a first early sampling dedicated to God, this Offering of the "Firstfruits" *sanctified* the whole Harvest to the Lord, and served as the *guarantee* of those blessings and fruitfulness which were to come.

The special Offering of the Wave-sheaf of Firstfruits during the Passover or Feast of Unleavened Bread is actually the ***prelude*** to the Pentecostal celebration with its own special Offering which would be offered in a similar fashion of being waved in the air. From the time of the Offering of this Firstfruit waved before the Lord, the Jewish people were to count 50 days till the Feast of Pentecost. This counting consisted of "seven weeks" (49 days) and then on the next day (the 50th day) the celebration would take place. This celebration consisted of the two Wave-loaves of Bread offered in a similar manner. These two special Offerings, the Wave-sheaf sample and the two Wave-loaves of Bread are, therefore, vitally connected. The Firstfruits Offering at Passover was a ***sampling*** of the full spring Harvest to be celebrated 50 days later at Pentecost (Lev. 23:9–16). Likewise, the second Offering was performed in a similar manner as the Wave-sheaf Offering 50 days earlier. In this regard the Feast of Firstfruits (Pentecost) appeared to be a conclusion to the Feast of Unleavened Bread (Passover). Because of this vital connection between the two Offerings, Pentecost was more commonly called *Azereth* (Conclusion) by the Jewish people. This was its most popular name in use among them.

The standard *Pentateuch & Haftorahs* which is read throughout the Jewish world today (edited by Dr. J.H. Hertz), says on page 521 concerning this relationship:

> The paragraph (Lev. 23:15–22) dealing with the Feast of Weeks [Pentecost] has no introductory formula . . . such as we find in connection with the other Festivals, because it was conceived as the complement of the Passover, and not something independent of it. Its name in Talmudic literature is not Shavuos, but almost invariably 'The Concluding Festival' to Passover.

The rabbinic name was therefore given as *Hag ha-Azereth*, or simply *Azereth*, meaning "The Feast of Conclusion."

Various Names for Pentecost

Because of the several different names given to the Feast of Pentecost, it would be good to list each one and give its distinctive meaning. In each case I will first give the Hebrew name and then the English translation.

1. *Hag ha-Katsir*, meaning "**Feast of the Harvest**." The fuller text says—"The Feast of the Harvest of the Firstfruits" (Exo. 23:16). Some would say simply the "Harvest Festival." In this regard it was also sometimes known as "The Feast of the First Harvest." This means there would also be the later fall Harvest Festival at the time of the Feast of Tabernacles.
2. *Hag ha-Bikurim*, meaning "**Feast of Firstfruits**." This is also taken from the same text of Exo. 23:16 because it was the harvest of the Firstfruits in view (see also Exo. 34:22). Because this Feast lasted only one day it is also called *Yom ha-Bikurim*, meaning "**Day of the Firstfruits**" (so it is stated in Num. 28:26). It is also referred to as "the Bread of the Firstfruits" (Lev 23:20). Because of the failure in many Bible translations to differentiate between *mo'adim* (appointed times) and *haggim* (festivals),

many teachers have erroneously called the Offering of the Wave-sheaf of firstfruits during Passover, "The Feast of Firstfruits." To my knowledge this is never done in Jewish literature. "The Feast of Firstfruits" is actually the same as the Feast of Pentecost in the Scriptures.

3. *Hag ha-Shavuot*, or simply *Shavuot*, meaning "**Feast of Weeks.**" The fuller passage says—"Feast of Weeks, the firstfruits of the wheat harvest" (Exo. 34:22, see also Num. 28:26 and Deut. 16:10 and 16). This name is derived from the counting of seven weeks after the Offering of the Firstfruit sample at Pentecost. This is the popular name of this Feast in Judaism today.

4. *Hag ha-Azereth*, or simply *Azereth*, meaning "**Feast of Conclusion.**" This is a later Rabbinic name used more commonly by the Jewish people than was the word *Pentecost*. As stated earlier, because of the vital connection of this Feast to what occurred before at Passover, the Feast was described as if it was the "conclusion" or the final day of the Feast of Unleavened Bread.

5. *Pentekostos* (Greek), translated "**Pentecost,**" which is simply the Anglicized form of the Greek word for 50th. This is its common designation in the book of Acts and 1 Corinthians (Acts 2:1; 20:16 and 1 Cor. 16:8). It is obviously the name given because of its celebration on the "fiftieth day" after the Offering of the Wave-sheaf at Passover.

6. *Hag Mator Torahteinu*, meaning "**Feast of the Giving of our Law** (Torah)." As noted earlier, this stems from the tradition of the Pharisees to connect *Shavuot* to the giving of the Law at Sinai. In this regard it was also sometimes called the "Festival of Revelation." As I stated earlier, this name was not used until a few hundred years after the Pentecost of Acts 2:1.

Alfred Edersheim in his book *"The Temple, Its Ministry and Services,"* (page 262) informs us that several of these names for the Feast such as "Feast of Weeks (*Shavuos*)," "Pentecost (50th)" and the early Jewish traditional name of "Feast of Conclusion (*Azereth*)" "all bear reference to this interval [of time] from the Passover." These names are numbers 3, 4 and 5 just mentioned. And indeed, they demonstrate the unique position of the Feast in relationship to the previous Offering of the Firstfruit at Passover.

In addition, it should be noted that the first two names for Pentecost (1 and 2) also demonstrate their relationship to the "Firstfruits" offering at Passover. *Hag ha-Katsir* means "the Harvest Feast" (of the Firstfruits harvest, Exo. 23:16) and *Yom ha-Bikurim* means "The Day of the Firstfruits" of the harvest (Num. 28:26).

Therefore, all these primary names for Pentecost (numbers 1-5), wherein the final Offering of the two Wave-loaves of bread is made, show and demonstrate their vital relationship to the special Wave-sheaf Offering at Passover.

"Christ the Firstfruits" (1 Cor. 15:20–23)

In 1 Corinthians 15:23 the resurrection of Jesus Christ is specifically identified as the antitype fulfillment of the "Wave-sheaf Offering" of the "Firstfruits" which took place at the Feast of Unleavened Bread (Passover). Paul, for emphasis, stated twice in this passage that Christ's resurrection was the fulfillment of the Firstfruit Offering. In verse 20, Paul said, "But now is Christ risen from the dead, and has become the *firstfruits* of those who have fallen asleep."

It is important just here to review the prophetic meaning or symbolism of this "Firstfruits Offering." As demonstrated before, it was originally offered on a Sunday morning during the Feast of Passover. As stated in all four Gospel accounts, Sunday morning was the time of Christ's resurrection from the dead. This was also the exact time of this particular Offering. It bears the following symbolism—

1. The initial planting of the seemingly dead kernels of grain serves as a picture of *death*. Christ said in John 12:24 "except a grain of wheat falls into the ground and *dies* . . ." In addition, Paul said, "What you sow is not made alive unless it *dies*" (1 Cor. 15:36).
2. The springing up of the new stalks of grain and their harvesting in the spring is understood by everyone as speaking of the *resurrection of the dead*. Christ stated in John 12:24

concerning His resurrection, "but if it dies, *it produces* [by springing to life] *much grain.*"
3. The ritual harvesting of the first early sampling of grain during the Feast of Unleavened Bread speaks of Christ's resurrection from the dead as the "Firstfruit" *sample* of the greater full harvest of those to also be raised from the dead. "But now is Christ *risen from the dead,* and has become the *Firstfruits* of *those who have fallen asleep*" (1 Cor. 15:20, 23).
4. The ritual waving of the first bundle of grain up in the air before God speaks of Christ's *ascension* up to the Father in heaven. In the Temple ritual this offering is in no way sacrificed, destroyed or burned; it is simply waved up in the air before God as if to be taken by Him.
5. This special offering of the early grain stands as a *token guarantee* of the greater harvest to be celebrated some 50 days later. "But if the Spirit of Him Who raised Jesus from the dead dwells in you, He Who *raised Christ from the dead* will also *give life to your mortal bodies through His Spirit* Who dwells in you . . . we also *who have the Firstfruits of the Spirit* . . . wait for the *redemption* of our body" (Rom. 8:11 and 23).

I do not believe that any serious student of the Bible would disagree with this basic understanding of the "Firstfruit Offering." This offering actually represents the very basis of the Christian faith and our purpose for service (1 Cor. 15:14–19). *"If Christ be not risen, our faith is vain"* (1 Cor. 15:14).

The importance of this first offering is further demonstrated by the command in the Law that no bread, parched grain or even fresh grain from the early harvest was to be eaten at the beginning of this new year until the day of this special offering (Lev. 23:14). This illustrates for us the spiritual truth that there is absolutely no hope or reality of life, either spiritually or physically, apart from the life imparted through the resurrection of Jesus Christ from the dead.

Concerning the fact that in this offering there was an actual measure or bundle of grain waved in the air, instead of just a single grain stalk, is very suggestive of the reality that at the time of Christ's resurrection there were numerous other saints in the city of Jerusalem who were also raised from the dead to give further verification to God's people of Christ's resurrection—see Matthew 27:51–53. Their "graves were opened" at the time of Christ's death, but they were not raised from the dead until after Christ's resurrection. Therefore, it is fitting that they were represented as a part of that bundle of grain waved up in the air.

"Counting of Days"

To continue the quote from the standard *Pentateuch & Haftorahs,* (page 521)—

> [Concerning Lev. 23:15] Talmudic literature [says]... 'We count the days that pass since the preceding Festival, just as one who expects his most intimate friend on a certain day counts the days and even the hours....' 'Unto you' [from the text of Lev. 23:15]. From this addition, the Rabbis deduce that each Israelite had the duty of counting for himself;... The season between Passover and Shavuos (or Pentecost which in Greek means 'the fiftieth day' after the first day of Passover) is known as *Sephirah*, Period of Counting.

"Indeed, the very command to count instructs us to establish a connection between the two periods," (Shlomo Reskin, *International Edition, Jerusalem Post,* "Count on freedom").

Beginning with the day of the Offering of the Wave-sheaf of Firstfruits (originally on a Sunday) the people were to count seven Sabbaths equaling 49 days. Then the next day would be another Sunday, the 50th day on which the Feast of Firstfruits (Pentecost) was held. I repeat again that this has also been called "Feast of Weeks" because of the seven weeks counted off. It has been more commonly called "Pentecost" (Fiftieth) in the Greek translation because it was celebrated on the 50th day.

Jewish tradition tells us that usually at the first meal of every day during those weeks the father would announce what day it was, such as "day one" or "day twenty," etc. In addition they would announce the week. Sometimes there might be certain prayers and Scriptures read during each of these weeks. This counting process caused everyone to look forward to the Feast which was to come. Truly, the "Conclusion" was greatly anticipated after all this counting.

Significance of the Number 50

The number 50 is also important in the Bible as to its spiritual significance. Obviously, the counting of fifty days gave an aura of *mystery* and *expectancy* for this particular Feast. The "countdown," so to speak, kept the attention and expectation of the people focused on the blessings of the early summer harvest. This was the only Feast which had such a "countdown."

The most popularly known use of the number 50 was in the great Jubilee year celebration. According to the Law, once the people of Israel came into their land they were to count off 49 years, and on the 50th year there was a great celebration and *release*. Those Jews who had sold themselves into slavery were automatically *freed* on that year. The lands of ancestral families, which had to be sold because of poverty, were sold with the amount of time remaining until the Jubilee year *"discounted"* or reckoned in the purchase price. Those who had sold properties could thus *return to them* in the Jubilee year. Now the Hebrew word for "Jubilee" is derived from the idea of "a joyful shout or trumpet blast." This was because the Jubilee year was announced by the special sound of a trumpet. This trumpet was to be blown on the Day of Atonement of the fiftieth year (Lev. 25:8–17 and 39, 40). Interestingly enough, the fiftieth day, as it relates to the prophetic aspect of the Feast of Pentecost, will be announced by a *trumpet sound* as well—see 1 Thessalonians 4:16 and 1 Corinthians 15:52.

The numerical value of 50 is basically derived by the counting of seven weeks of years or days, whichever is in view. 7 times 7 equals 49. As the number seven is used in the Scriptures, it is generally recognized as the factor of *"completion"* as in the week of creation.

In Genesis chapter two, verses one and two, we read, "Thus the heavens and the earth, and all the host of them were *finished*. And on the seventh day God *ended* His work which He had done, . . ." The two words *"finished"* and *"ended"* give us the meaning of *"completion."* In turn, this is the idea affixed to the spiritual implications of the use of the number "seven" in the Bible. This is illustrated again in the last book of the Bible where we have a series of sevens. There are "letters to the seven churches," "seven seals," "seven trumpets," "seven thunders" and the "seven bowls." Each of these "sevens" *completes* a section or a subject during the period of Great Tribulation as described in the pages of this book. So again the idea of *completion* is encompassed in the numerical value of seven.

In turn, seven sevens would simply represent *"Perfect Completion."* The added number of one to total 50 makes it representative of the *"Divine (1), Perfect (7X) Consummation or Completion (7) of Time."* Thus, the arrival of the 50th year or the 50th day was greatly anticipated as arranged and ordered by God. The 50th year or 50th day celebration simply commemorated the God-ordained *fullness* or *completion* of time for whichever purpose God assigned to it. Especially was this true for the first agricultural Harvest Feast celebration. So the number 50, as used in the Bible, simply signifies *"fullness"* or *"completion,"* especially the idea of *"Divine, perfect completion."* E. W. Bullinger in his book *Number In Scripture*, states on page 268, regarding the use of the number 50: "[50] points to deliverance and rest following as the result of the *perfect consummation of time."*

Obviously, I will have more to say about this aspect of Pentecost later in this study. Suffice it to say here, that as this Feast will be used to prophetically portray the future harvesting of the righteous dead of the Church Age, the number 50 simply points to the specified time of *"fullness or completion"* which is to be determined alone by the divine counsel of God. It most certainly does not symbolize a literal 50 years transpiring until their resurrection. The number "50" as used in the Scriptures simply signifies "fullness or completion" for the designated purpose, *no matter what the actual time in days or years may be.*

Chapter Six

The PARAKLETOS OF PENTECOST

Uniqueness of Pentecost

As I previously mentioned, it is noteworthy that the Feast of Pentecost, or *"Shavuot,"* as it is called by the Jewish people today, was different from the other two Feasts in one distinctive way. The other Feasts were associated with some specific event in Israel's historic beginning. The Feast of Unleavened Bread (or Passover) commemorated Israel's deliverance out of Egypt (Exo. 13:3, etc.) and the Feast of Ingathering or Tabernacles commemorated Israel's dwelling in booths for forty years during their wilderness journey (Lev. 23:42, 43). However, the Feast of Pentecost was not connected to any historical event in Israel's beginning as revealed through Moses. In this regard, it stood simply as a parenthetical one day Feast situated between the other two major Feasts of seven and eight days each.

Some Jewish writers who describe their Holy Days take note of this fact. One states, "Shavuot differs from the other two festivals in that a specific historical observance is not mentioned in the Torah; it was only later tradition that identified it with Moses and Sinai." (From *Celebrating the Jewish Holidays,* a Friedman Group Production, page 116). As stated earlier, it was in much later tradition that the Pharisees linked the Feast of Firstfruits (Pentecost) with Moses giving the Law from Mount Sinai. However, this is not specifically indicated or stated in the Law of Moses. It was simply a much later tradition in an effort to connect the Feast to something tangible in Israel's early history.

It appears, therefore, that when we avoid this later, added Jewish tradition, this Feast of Firstfruits lent itself to a different time period altogether. In fact, this parenthetical setting makes the Feast of Pentecost all the more *applicable* to the present Church Age, which is also *parenthetical* in nature.

The Parakletos of Pentecost

The one thing that Jesus Christ, Himself, did associate with Pentecost was none other than the coming of the Holy Spirit to take up His residence upon this earth in the lives of all God's people who had been saved through the blood of Christ. This was something that Christ was very concerned and particular about. He prepared the apostles and disciples beforehand by giving them many clear statements and explanations, the first of which was recorded for us in John 14:16–18—

> And I [Christ] will pray the Father, and He will give you another Helper [*Parakletos*] that He may abide with you forever—the Spirit of truth; Whom the world cannot receive, because it neither sees Him nor knows Him; but you know Him, for He dwells with you and will be in you. I will not leave you orphans; I will come to you.

As to the meaning of *Parakletos*, perhaps the explanation by W. E. Vine in *The Expanded Vine's Expository Dictionary of New Testament Words* best expresses it:

> ... a calling to one's side (*para,* beside, *kaleo,* to call); ... i.e., to one's aid, is primarily a verbal adjective, and suggests the capability of adaptability for giving aid. It was used in a court of justice to denote

a legal assistant, counsel for the defense, an advocate; then, generally, one who pleads another's case, an intercessor, advocate, as in 1 John 2:1, of the Lord Jesus. In the widest sense, it signifies a succourer, comforter. Christ was this to His disciples, by implication of the word 'another Comforter,' when speaking of the Holy Spirit, . . .

Further, in John 14:26 Christ stated—

But the Helper [*Parakletos*], the Holy Spirit, Whom the Father will send in My name, He will teach you all things, and bring to your remembrance all things that I said to you.

Again, in John 15:26 Christ stated—

But when the Helper [*Parakletos*] comes, Whom I shall send to you from the Father, the Spirit of truth Who proceeds from the Father, He will testify of Me.

In John 16:7–15 we have this additional revelation—

Nevertheless I tell you the truth, it is to your advantage that I go away; for if I do not go away, the Helper [*Parakletos*] will not come to you; but if I depart, I will send Him to you. And when He has come, He will convict the world of sin, and of righteousness, and of judgment: of sin, because they do not believe in Me; of righteousness, because I go to My Father and you see Me no more; of judgment, because the ruler of this world is judged. I still have many things to say to you, but you cannot bear them now. However, when He, the Spirit of truth, has come, He will guide you into all truth; for He will not speak on His own authority, but whatever He hears He will speak; and He will tell you things to come. He will glorify Me, for He will take of what is Mine and declare it to you. All things that the Father has are Mine. Therefore I said that He will take of Mine and declare it to you.

Then, after Christ's resurrection from the dead, just before His ascension up to the Father, and just ten days before Pentecost, Christ said as recorded in Luke 24:49—

Behold, I send the Promise of My Father upon you, but tarry in the city of Jerusalem until you are endued with power from on high [at Pentecost].

And then the words of Christ on this occasion are further recorded by Luke in Acts 1:4 and 5—

And being assembled together with them, He commanded them not to depart from Jerusalem, but to wait for the Promise of the Father, 'which,' He said, 'you have heard from Me; for John truly baptized with water, but you shall be baptized with the Holy Spirit not many days [10 days, to be exact] from now.'

And finally, Christ explained that, in essence, this "promised" baptism of the Holy Spirit is not that which is yet to come in the setting up of Israel's earthly Kingdom. Acts 1:6–8—

Therefore, when they had come together, they asked Him, saying, 'Lord, will you at this time restore the Kingdom to Israel?' And He said to them, 'It is not for you to know times and seasons which the Father has put in His own authority. But you shall receive power when the Holy Spirit has come upon you; and you shall be witnesses to Me in Jerusalem, and in all Judea and Samaria, and to the end of the earth.'

Please remember that the prophets repeatedly prophesied of a coming outpouring of the Holy Spirit in the future Messianic

Kingdom age (Isa. 32:15; 44:3; Ezek. 36:25-33; 39:29 and Joel 2:28). This will take place when Messiah reigns on earth. This baptism was especially related to the great blessings that God had in store for the Jewish nation at the time of its national conversion, but it would also spill over into all the earth. However, this is not the baptism of the Holy Spirit which Christ privately began to promise to the apostles and disciples on the night of His betrayal. This promised baptism of the Holy Spirit, which references I have quoted above, was actually in lieu of Israel having rejected her own Messiah. This baptism would take place after Christ left the earth and went into heaven to be seated at the right hand of the Father. In the interim, between Christ's rejection and His second coming to actually reign on earth, there is the present spiritual Kingdom of God (Rom. 14:17 and Col. 1:13). On the Day of Pentecost when Peter preached to the crowd of Jews who had gathered, his explanation for the phenomenal work of the Spirit in the gift of tongues was that it was the same Holy Spirit Who was to come, as prophesied by Joel. However, Peter did not say the prophecy of Joel 2 was actually literally fulfilled, but rather that "this is that . . . Spirit" spoken of in Joel–Acts 2:16, 17).

Now, the actual inauguration of this present spiritual Kingdom was by the baptism of the Holy Spirit on the Day of Pentecost. In addition, the Holy Spirit, now in residence upon this earth in the lives of believers, actually *directs* in the affairs of the Church of Jesus Christ—see Acts 2:4; 5:9; 6:10; 8:29; 8:39; 10:19; 11:12; 11:28; 16:7; 20:22, etc. In fact, this Church Age can be properly and literally designated as being under *"the administration of the Spirit"* (2 Corinthians 3:8, 9, literal translation).

The Administration of the Spirit

Because the Holy Spirit has taken up His residence upon this earth in the lives of believers, some Bible teachers have even called this age, "The Dispensation of the Spirit." It is evident from several Scriptures that the Holy Spirit is acting as the director or administrator of Christ's spiritual Kingdom in the world today (Rom. 14:17). In contrast to the "ministration" of the Law, Paul says, "How shall not *the ministration of the Spirit* be more glorious?" (2 Cor. 3:8.)

The Greek word for "ministration" here is *diakonia*, which actually has to do with "the office and work of a *diakonos* [minister]" (W. E. Vine). It is to be understood as an administration or, as translated in the King James, "ministration."

Jesus, in talking to the woman at the well in John 4, described this coming age as a time when "true worshipers will worship the Father *in Spirit and truth*, for the Father is seeking such to worship Him. *God is Spirit*, and those who worship Him must worship *in Spirit and truth*" (John 4:23, 24). Paul spoke to the Church with these words—"Blessed be the God and Father of our Lord Jesus Christ, Who has blessed us with every *spiritual blessing* in the heavenly places in Christ" (Eph. 1:3), and said that every believer has been "*sealed with the Holy Spirit of Promise*" (Eph. 1:13). Again, Paul said of the collective body of Christ, "In Whom [Christ] the whole building, being fitted together, grows into *a holy temple in the Lord*, in Whom you also are being built together for a *dwelling place of God by the Spirit*" (Eph. 2:21, 22).

It is interesting that some of those, who do not believe Pentecost could ever actually be typical of the Church of Jesus Christ, will nevertheless answer, when asked "What then was Pentecost typical of?"—"Why, of course," they say, "It was typical of the Holy Spirit." This is the answer by Terry C. Hubert when he gave his doctoral thesis entitled *The Eschatological Significance of Israel's Annual Feasts,* which was put forth by Thomas Ice in his paper entitled *Israel's Fall Feasts and date-setting of the Rapture.* This is also stated by others of the Dallas Theological seminary, such as Roy B. Zuck (see *Basic Bible Interpretation,* page 180). Now this is an amazing admission! If Pentecost is typical of the Holy Spirit, then it must be the Holy Spirit Who "baptized" the believers on the Day of Pentecost. And I must add, it is the same Holy Spirit Who continued to "baptize" the new Gentile converts under Peter's ministry (Acts 10:44–46; 11:16, 17). In addition, it must be the same Holy Spirit, of Whom it is said, "For by one Spirit ARE WE ALL BAPTIZED INTO ONE BODY—whether Jews or Gentiles, whether slaves or free—and have all been made to drink into one Spirit" (1 Cor. 12:13). So it is, that all believers in the Age of Grace get the Pentecostal experience of the baptism of the Holy Spirit into the body of Christ. So it is the Holy Spirit Who is building the Church which is Christ's body.

Consequently, the only sense in which Pentecost is typical of the Holy Spirit is precisely because of the *unique work* the Holy Spirit is doing in this particular age! Christ is creating the Church by means of the Holy Spirit. The Holy Spirit specifically *"baptizes"* all believers into the one body of Jesus Christ. The Holy Spirit is then the *"administrator"* of this age. He *directed* in all the affairs of the early Church. He blesses us with all *"spiritual blessings* in heavenly places in Christ" (Eph. 1:3). This is also the same Holy Spirit Who guarantees the resurrection of the Church (Rom. 8:11) by giving us "the Firstfruits of the Spirit." He is the same Holy Spirit Who is understood to be "taken out of the midst" at the close of this age so that the Antichrist might be revealed (2 Thess. 2:7). Thus it is that the Holy Spirit vitalizes the Church of Jesus Christ, and to say "Pentecost was typical of the Holy Spirit" is to acknowledge that Pentecost was typical of the Church which was so vitalized by the Holy Spirit.

This is the same Holy Spirit of Whom Alfred Edersheim, the renowned Hebrew Christian scholar wrote in his book *The Temple, Its Ministry and Services*, on pages 266 and 267—

> For, as the worshipers were in the Temple, probably just as they were offering the wave-lambs and the wave-bread, the multitude heard that 'sound from heaven, as of a mighty rushing wind,' which drew them to the house where the apostles were gathered, there to hear 'every man in his own language' 'the wonderful works of God.'

Thus, the waving of the two loaves of bread, the "New grain Offering," up in the air marked the precise time (about 9:00 A. M., Acts 2:15) of the birth of the "One New man" (Eph. 2:15) of this present Church Age.

"When The Day Of Pentecost Was Fully Come"

In the second chapter of the book of Acts we are to understand that the "counting of days" had been completed. Remember, the Jewish day always begins with sunset in the evening. Seven weeks had passed and at the evening meal beginning this day, the heads of homes had usually announced to the household, "This is the fiftieth day."

The next morning (at the time of the Wave-loaves Offering) "the Day of Pentecost (50th) had *fully come*" (Acts 2:1). It is interesting to note a literal translation of this verse. The Greek word (*sumpleroo*) translated "fully come" is literally a compound word meaning, *sum*, "to fill," and *pleroo*, "completely"—specifically, "to fill completely." The Greek word for "fully" or "fullness" is *pleroma*, and is a synonym to *sumpleroo*, yet it is actually only the last half of the word. Therefore, a very literal translation of this verse should be "When the Day of Pentecost *was fully completed*." The NASB Interlinear Greek-English New Testament renders it simply "completed." This translation does two things: first, it ties in the fact that the "counting of days" had been "completed"; second, it demonstrates the fact of the spiritual significance of the number 50, which, as I pointed out before, signifies *"fullness* or *completion"*—divine, perfect completion.

In addition, this translation also reflects upon the Jewish tradition of commonly calling this Feast "The Feast of Conclusion (*Hag ha-Azereth*)." This is the Feast which "concludes" or "completes" the earlier Feast of Unleavened Bread when the priest offered the "Wave-sheaf of Firstfruits." Jewish sages noted that the Feast of Tabernacles was said to be a Feast of "seven days" (Lev. 23:34), yet there was an "eighth day" added to it which was also a High Sabbath (Lev. 23:39). Therefore, these rabbis also thought that Shavout (Pentecost) should be considered as merely the "Conclusion (*Azereth*)," or the "eighth day" of the Feast of Unleavened Bread. This was actually said to be a very common designation of Pentecost used by the Jewish people during the New Testament times and thereafter.

The first thing on schedule in the Temple on this Sunday morning was a *"New Grain Offering"* in the form of two loaves of bread to be waved up in the air, just as the handful or stalks of early spring grain were waved up in the air 50 days earlier. This day was a special High Sabbath. This was the second Feast on Israel's liturgical calendar where all the males, from 20 years old and upward, were required to be present in Jerusalem before the Lord (Exo. 23:14–17 and Deut. 16:16).

The Jewish brethren, who formed the early community of believers in Jesus Christ as Israel's Messiah, had also congregated for united prayer and Pentecostal celebration at or near the Temple area. It was about 9:00 A.M. Sunday morning (Acts 2:1 and 15). There was a suspense in their anticipation, for Christ had promised that the Holy Spirit would soon come! Would it be then? And it was!

The "New Grain Offering"

In the Temple court the priests were presenting the "New Grain Offering" which was customarily done the first thing in the morning. As we shall see, the very name of this Offering made it unique from all others. Antitypically, we must remember that this Offering symbolized the work of the Holy Spirit in starting a whole new grain field as was stated at the beginning of this book (chapter one). Actually, this Offering was the highlight of this particular Feast. In addition, there would be many other offerings to accompany this Offering. The instructions about this grain offering were followed with meticulous care. The spring maturing of the grain normally began with the barley (see Exo. 9:31, 32 and Ruth 1:22). The first early barley which had ripened enough was usually taken for the "Firstfruit Offering" at the time of the Feast of Unleavened Bread. Then the final early summer harvesting of the grain, which was celebrated fifty days later, would usually take place either during or at the conclusion of the wheat harvest (Ruth 2:23). At the Feast of Pentecost the waving of the "New Grain Offering" was made. I will list the sequences in this Offering and give the spiritual symbolism.

1. Of course, the kernels of grain had been planted many months before as the winter wheat or barley planting. The planting of these seemingly dead kernels of grain in the ground was a picture

of *death* as stated by Christ, Himself (John 12:24). Now these kernels of grain so planted speak specifically of those who *"have fallen asleep in Christ"* (1 Cor. 15:18, 20 and 1 Thess. 4:13).
2. As previously stated, the growth, ripening and harvesting of the wheat clearly speak of and symbolize the *resurrection* of the dead *"in Christ"* (John 12:24 and 1 Cor. 15:23). I will add to this the testimony of 1 Cor. 15:35–38,

> But if someone will say, '*How are the dead raised up? And with what body do they come?*' Foolish one, what you sow is not made alive unless it dies. And what you sow, you do not sow that body that shall be, but mere grain— perhaps wheat or some other grain. But God gives it a body as He pleases, and to each seed its own body.

3. After the 49 days had been counted, the wheat planting was usually already in the process of being harvested. This crop is called the *"Harvest of Firstfruits"* (Exo. 23:16, etc.) of the year. Jewish custom indicates that just before the 50th day, a number of the priests certified that some of the best grain had been selected and prepared in a proper manner according to the Law. This grain would be an amount large enough to make two loaves of bread. This selected grain would represent the whole harvest of Firstfruits. In this case it would represent what has been called *"the universal Church"*—*"the Church which is Christ's body"* (Eph. 1:22, 23). This offering would typify the truth of 1 Thessalonians 4:14—"For if we believe that Jesus died and *rose again,* even so [or *in like manner*] God will bring with Him [in resurrection] those who sleep in Jesus."
4. After the stalks of grain chosen for this particular offering were harvested, they were NOT offered up in their raw natural state as was done in the earlier Firstfruit Offering at the Passover. In this case the grain was threshed or beaten out and ground into fine flour. The flour was all mingled and kneaded together into one large batch of dough. Kneading is defined as "to mix and work a substance into a uniform mass, by folding, pressing, stretching

and shaping." This grinding of grain and kneading together into one batch was typical of the Holy Spirit's work of "baptizing" all believers together into *"one body"* and *"one bread"* (1 Cor. 12:13 and 10:17), *"whether they be Jews or Gentiles, whether slaves or free . . . male or female . . . for we are all partakers of that one bread"* (1 Cor. 12:13; Gal. 3:28 and 1 Cor. 10:17).

5. The addition of "leaven" to make the bread rise was normal in the process of making bread as a wholesome food, and can simply speak of rapid growth—in this case the "rising" and growth of the Church of Jesus Christ. Many have supposed that since elsewhere leaven is used as symbolic of sin, the same must be the case here. This may or may not be true. However, I quite frankly am suspicious of that interpretation because this bread is offered up to God as the workmanship of the Holy Spirit in the believer during this Age. Naturally, this "bread" is not to be confused with mere "Christendom" with all its hypocrisies and characteristic blasphemies. Rather, it is the real "bread" of God's people saved during this present Age of Grace.

6. The "New Grain or New Meal Offering" (Lev. 23:16), as it is designated by the Spirit of God, speaks of the Church of our Lord Jesus Christ as a *"New Creation"* (2 Cor. 5:17) and as becoming *"One New Man"* (Eph. 2:15). Thus, the designation for this special offering fits perfectly God's inspired description of the Church of Jesus Christ.

7. The batch of dough was large enough to make two loaves of bread which simply speaks of *double fruitfulness*. Some interpreters think this is representative of the Jew and Gentile believers in the Church. However, in this case the Jew and the Gentile are already mixed together as one entity, making *"one new man."* Consequently, the two loaves are not different substances, but are of the same substance.

8. The baking of this bread in the fires of the oven speaks, of course, of the trials and testing which actually cause this bread to bake into a rich, wholesome food ready to be served. The apostle Peter alludes to the value of the believer's testing "by fire" in his first epistle. Please see 1 Peter 1:3–9. Not every believer is exposed directly to the same amount of the fire. The outside edges are

directly exposed to the fire or heat, whereas the inside bears only the radiation.

9. It was customary that in the morning of this High Sabbath of Pentecost the two loaves of bread, freshly baked, were taken into the Temple court for the presentation. During the ceremony these two loaves of bread were *waved from side to side and up in the air*, passing over the head of the priest. This speaks, as did the "Firstfruit" Offering 50 days earlier, of *ascension*—as it were, up to God!

10. The whole ritual is said to be *"before the Lord"* (Lev. 23:20). That means it goes to God and is for God. It represents a special offering, ascending up to the Father in heaven. It is as if the Lord in heaven would reach down and take it from the hands of the priest. It would represent food for the Lord, and therefore only a designated priest would take it.

11. This Offering was accompanied by all the various sacrificial offerings that the Law demanded (see Lev. 23:18–20). These sacrificial offerings speak of the various, totally completed and satisfactory works of our Lord Jesus Christ in His substitutionary death and resurrection for us. Christ's atoning work, in all its various ramifications, is the basis for our total salvation and presentation before the Lord.

12. As we have testified before, this offering was made on the morning of the 50th day. The number 50 signifies *fullness* or *completion*. (We will have more to say about the prophetic aspect of this number shortly.) At approximately 9:00 o'clock in the morning hour this offering was made and at that time the Holy Spirit took up His residence upon the earth. See again, *The Temple its Ministry and Services* by Alfred Edersheim, pages 266 and 267. Edersheim indicates that the sound as a "rushing mighty wind" was the outward sign or manifestation of the arrival of the Holy Spirit on earth, baptizing all believers into one new body— "The Church Which Is Christ's Body." Thus God coordinated the birth of the Church with the morning "New Grain Offering" of the Feast of Pentecost.

As to the fulfillment of the prophetic aspect of this offering, we can first of all remember by the earlier example, that when the *"fullness of time"* (Gal. 4:4, 5) came for Christ's redemptive work in His glorious resurrection, God coordinated the Sunday morning offering of the *"Firstfruit Wave Offering"* with Christ's resurrection from the dead and His ascension into heaven. So it shall be at the end of this Age. When the *"fullness of the Gentiles"* comes (Rom. 11:25), God will coordinate what the *"New Grain Offering"* typified in resurrection and ascension, with its prophetic fulfillment in the resurrection and Rapture of the Church into heaven.

Keep in mind that the number 50 symbolizes *completion or fullness,* and when this happens for the Church, it is not to be relegated or governed by anything in Israel's history, not even the date of Pentecost on the calendar. It stands parenthetical in nature, and relative only to the symbolic meaning of "50," which is in the determination of God as to that "fullness."

Chapter Seven

PROPHETIC ASPECT OF PENTECOST

Prophetic Character derived from the Wave-sheaf at Passover

The Feast of Pentecost receives its whole character from the previous Wave-sheaf Offering at Passover. In *Chapter Five—PRELUDE TO PENTECOST*—it was carefully demonstrated that most of the names for Pentecost are derived from the earlier very special Wave-sheaf Offering at Passover.

Hag ha-Katzir, "Feast of Harvest," is derived from the first early sample of the harvest—the "Offering of the Omer" or the "Wave-sheaf" at Passover.

Hag ha-Bikurim, "Feast of Firstfruits," is derived from the first early sample which was also called the "Wave-sheaf of Firstfruits" of the early harvest.

Hag ha-Shavuot, "Feast of Weeks," is derived from the seven weeks which follow the Wave-sheaf Offering at Passover.

Hag ha-Azereth, "Feast of Conclusion," is derived from Pentecost being the concluding one day festival to Passover (the Feast of Unleavened Bread).

Pentekostos (Greek), "Pentecost," is derived from the number 50, being 50 days after the Wave-sheaf Offering at Passover.

The Feast of Pentecost, therefore, receives all its primary characteristics from the earlier very important Wave-sheaf Offering of Firstfruits at Passover. (1) The **name** of Pentecost as "Feast of Firstfruits" is derived from the sample of *Firstfruits* previously offered. (2) The **time** upon which Pentecost was to be observed derives from the *day* the Wave-sheaf was offered. (3) The **character** of Pentecost being a Firstfruit Harvest Festival is derived from the earlier Firstfruit Harvest *sample*. (4) The nature of the **two loaves of bread** Offering at Pentecost is derived from the early sample *Grain Offering*. (5) The **waving** of the Offering up in the air is derived from, and similar in action to, the *waving* up in the air of the early sample of the Wave-sheaf at Passover.

Therefore, in a similar manner, it is most important to realize that what the earlier Wave-sheaf Offering of grain symbolized prophetically, namely, **the bodily resurrection of Christ from the dead**, is precisely what the Wave-loaves symbolized prophetically—namely, **the bodily resurrection of the whole body of Christ (the Church) from the dead.**

In *Chapter Six*, The PARAKLETOS OF PENTECOST, it was shown that all the **works** in this time period—the *creation* of the Church by the baptism of the Holy Spirit, the *ministry* of the Church in evangelism, the *director* in the affairs of the Church, the *very fruit* in the lives of individuals in the Church, the multitude of *spiritual blessings*, and the *guarantee* of the Church's bodily resurrection—are all done by the Holy Spirit of God, sent down to earth to embody Christ in us, beginning at Pentecost.

Now let us focus more carefully upon this prophetic aspect of Pentecost which most expositors have somehow missed—the Pentecostal Rapture of the Church.

The Prophetic Application
of This Feast to the Church by the Apostle Paul

I have stated from the beginning of this Bible study that the apostle Paul, the Apostle to the Gentiles, unquestionably applies certain parts of the language concerning this Harvest Feast of *Firstfruits* to the subject of *the resurrection and Rapture of the Church of Jesus Christ*. And if Paul does, then there should be no question about the fact that Pentecost has its full prophetic fulfillment at the Rapture. Now let us read slowly and carefully the following passages from the inspired pen of Paul. Let us think and meditate about what we read and ask God to illuminate our minds and hearts.

<u>First,</u>
1 Corinthians 15:20 and 23

"THOSE WHO ARE CHRIST'S at His coming"

> But now Christ is risen from the dead, and has become the *Firstfruits of those who have fallen asleep.*

> But each in his own order: Christ the *Firstfruits*, afterwards THOSE WHO ARE CHRIST'S *at His coming.*

Now, exactly what does this last verse mean? Of course, the context is clearly talking about the subject of *the resurrection of the dead*. In fact, the resurrection is the whole subject of this 15th chapter of 1 Corinthians. Paul spoke clearly of the importance of the resurrection of Jesus Christ. It is the basis of our faith. But not only that, it is also the *guarantee* of *our own resurrections from the dead*. In laying out this clear principle, Paul goes back in time and uses the typology of Israel's Feasts. Twice (vs. 20 and 23) he stated that Christ is the antitypical "Firstfruits" Offering, which took place at Passover.

But the essential fact about the "Firstfruits" Offering was that it is *typical* OF the whole "*Harvest of Firstfruits*," which is what the celebration of Pentecost represented. The first Offering at

Passover points forward to the celebration of Pentecost. In the very first chapter of this book it was clearly established that Pentecost was essentially a Harvest Festival. Therefore, in this case, Paul was first of all saying that Christ is the "Firstfruit" sample of the whole "Harvest." In particular, Paul said Christ is the "Firstfruits *OF* those who have fallen asleep." This is a clear reference to the *dead* of the Church of Jesus Christ. So, I say again, if Christ is the "*Firstfruits*" sample of "*those who have fallen asleep in Christ*," then these dead in Christ represent the *Church of Jesus Christ* whose members will be Harvested at the Rapture. Let us note Paul's words and compare them with the known Rapture passage of 1 Thessalonians 4—

(1) 1 Corinthians 15:20: ". . . and has become the Firstfruts of those who have *fallen asleep*"—". . . **those *who sleep* in Jesus**" (1 Thess. 4:14).
(2) 1 Corinthians 15:23: ". . . afterwards those who *are Christ's* . . ." —"**And the dead *in Christ* shall rise first**" (1 Thess. 4:16).
(3) 1 Corinthians 15:23: ". . . *at His coming*"—". . . **the *coming of the Lord* . . .**" (1 Thess. 4:1).

Twice in this passage from I Corinthians 15 (verses 20 and 23) Paul drew the *connection* between Christ as the antitypical "Firstfruit" sample of grain, which was offered at the time of the Passover Feast, with the ***Harvest*** it anticipated as being the members of the Church of Jesus Christ who have "*fallen asleep*" in Him. In other words, this is saying that Christ fulfills the "Firstfruit" typology by His resurrection and, likewise, the Church fulfills the "Harvest of Firstfruits" typology by its resurrection and/or Rapture.

To make sure we are not alone in seeing that the resurrections of both Christ and the saints of Christ (the Church) are in view in both of these Feasts, allow me to quote some of the standard commentaries on 1 Corinthians 15:20–23. I believe most commentaries would confirm this understanding. This shall emphasize that both Offerings, the Wave-sheaf and the Wave-loaves, are intended to typify RESURRECTION of the dead—both of Jesus Christ and of the Harvest to follow. So, in quoting these commentaries, I will emphasize in bold the resurrection theme—

Jamieson, Fausset and Brown, Commentary on the Whole Bible, by Zondervan, on 1 Corinthians 15:20: "The firstfruits—the earnest or pledge, that **the whole resurrection harvest will follow**, . . ." In addition, a later statement on 1 Corinthians 16:2 states: "The feast of the wave offering of the first sheaf, answering to the Lord's **resurrection**; Pentecost, or the feast of weeks typical of the fruits of **the resurrection in the Christian Church** . . . ."

The Bible Knowledge Commentary, by the Dallas Theological Seminary Faculty, on 1 Corinthians 15:20: "He is the *firstfruits,* an Old Testament word (e.g., Ex. 23:16, 19) here used in the sense of a preliminary installment of what [in resurrection] will be both an example and a guarantee of more to come (cf. Rom. 8:23)." And again on verse 23: "As He promised (John 14:2–3) Christ will return for those who compose the church and **the dead in Christ will be raised** (I Thess. 4:16)."

Barnes' Notes on the New Testament, on 1 Corinthians 15:20: "The word [firstfruits] , therefore, comes to have two senses, or to involve two ideas: (1) That which is *first*, the beginning, or that which has priority of time; and (2) that which is a part and portion of the whole which is to follow, and which is the earnest or pledge of that; as the first sheaf of ripe grain was not only the first in order of time, but was the earnest or pledge of the entire harvest which was soon to succeed. . . . as the first sheaf of the harvest was with the crop; He was a part of the mighty **harvest of the resurrection**, and **His rising** was a portion of **that great rising**, as the sheaf was a portion of the harvest itself; and He was so connected with them all, and **their rising** so depended on His, that **His resurrection** was a demonstration that **they would rise**."

The New Bible Commentary: Revised, on 1 Corinthians 15:20–28: "First fruits implies community of nature with the 'harvest' to follow; i.e., Christ's **resurrection** promises **the ultimate home-gathering** of all God's people. The full harvest was foreshadowed and consecrated by the first sheaf brought as an offering on the day following the Sabbath after the Passover (Lv. 23:10f.), . . ."

I believe this is more than sufficient to demonstrate that the standard biblical commentaries are united in recognizing that both offerings—the Firstfruit Wave-sheaf at Passover, and the Wave-loaves at Pentecost—symbolize the theme of the resurrection from the dead. Therefore, the Wave-loaves at Pentecost, like the Wave-sheaf at Passover, have a primary *prophetic significance* which is assigned to the theme of the resurrection of the dead. In the case of the Pentecostal Offering, it represents what we commonly call "the Rapture of the Church."

There is an interesting sideline note concerning the situation of Paul for making this revelation. This revelation was made by Paul to the Corinthians, and beyond them to "all who in every place call on the name of Jesus Christ our Lord" (1 Cor. 1:2). It was made about A.D. 56 as Paul wrote to the Corinthians from the city of Ephesus (Acts 19:21, 22 and 1 Cor. 4:17). Apparently Paul wrote at the time of *"Passover"* (1 Cor. 5:7, 8). Paul told the Corinthians that he intended to stay *"in Ephesus until Pentecost"* (1 Cor. 16:8). Consequently, we can observe that Paul's physical situation was somewhat similar to the spiritual revelation he was giving about these two Feasts. Interestingly enough, the revelation that Paul gave in these verses has the effect of telling the Church that it will not leave this world until the prophetic fulfillment of Pentecost!

Sometimes the simplicity and brevity of the inspired words will allow us to read quickly and superficially. Consequently, we do not appreciate the depth of meaning in what is being said unless we stop and *meditate* upon the Word as God desires that we do. When we realize the basis upon which Paul was writing, the significance of the truth will illuminate our hearts. The truth that Paul gave in 1 Corinthians 15:20 and 23 is clearly based upon the Law concerning the "Firstfruit Offering" of the "Wave-sheaf" and the following

Harvest Feast called "the Feast of Weeks or Firstfruits," better known to us as "Pentecost." This is found in Leviticus 23:10–17—

> He shall wave the **sheaf** [of Firstfruits] before the Lord [v. 11, **typical of** *Christ's resurrection and ascension*].
> Count fifty days to the day after the seventh Sabbath [v. 16] . . . [and] **two wave loaves** . . . . the Firstfruits to the Lord [v. 17, **typical of** *'they that are Christ's at His coming'*].

Christ's resurrection and ascension served as the "Firstfruits" token of the greater "Firstfruits" harvest to come. The resurrection and ascension of the Church of Jesus Christ *is the greater Harvest to come!* These are not difficult passages to understand. As I quoted before, it has been said, "Firstfruits implies community of nature with the 'harvest' to follow; i.e., Christ's resurrection promises *the ultimate home-gathering* of all Christ's people in this age. The full harvest was foreshadowed and consecrated by the first sheaf brought as an offering on the day following the Sabbath after Passover (Lev. 23:10f.)." *The New Bible Commentary: Revised,* Eerdmans.

The Day of Pentecost is, therefore, *prophetic* of the resurrection and ascension of the Church of Jesus Christ—i.e., what we commonly call "the Rapture." The Church was born on this prophetic Feast day which, as to its prophetic aspect, is yet to be fulfilled in the *Rapture of the Church of Jesus Christ* in the future. Amazing as it may seem, because of our realization of this revelation, we can now say, "This is a primary reason why the Church was born on Pentecost—to ultimately signify the Harvest, i.e., the Rapture!"

I have gone into a much more detailed examination of I Corinthians 15: 20–28 in the book entitled *The Threefold Order of The Resurrection of The Righteous*. I would encourage you to read that study as a further complement to this particular exposition which focuses upon the Feast of Pentecost.

In this regard, one should remember that in the I Corinthian 15:20–28 passage, Paul was inspired to reveal the various "orders" or "stages" in the resurrection of the righteous. The righteous, those who are saved and justified by faith in God's gracious provision for salvation, are all going to be resurrected from the dead—but not all at the same time. Paul reveals three such "orders"—". . . even so in Christ all shall be made alive. But each in his own **order**: [1] Christ the *Firstfruits*, [2] afterwards *those who are Christ's* at His coming. [3] Then *comes the end,* when . . . . The last enemy that will be destroyed is *death.*" (In my book, *The Threefold Order of the Resurrection of the Righteous,* I show that all the Old Testament and Tribulation saints are raised in this third "order.")

<u>Second,</u>
Leviticus 23:17— Romans 8:11 and 23

"FIRSTFRUITS to the LORD—the FIRSTFRUITS of the Spirit"

You shall bring from your dwellings two wave loaves of two-tenths of an ephah. They shall be of fine flour; they shall be baked with leaven. They are the **FIRSTFRUITS to the LORD** [Lev. 23:17].

But if the Spirit of Him Who raised Jesus from the dead *dwells in you,* He Who raised Christ from the dead will *also give life to your mortal bodies through His Spirit Who dwells in you.* . . . And not only that, but we also who have **the FIRSTFRUITS of the Spirit,** even we ourselves groan within ourselves, eagerly waiting for the adoption, *the redemption of our body* [Rom. 8:11 and 23].

The situation for Paul writing this epistle is also interesting. Paul wrote this epistle of Romans from the city of Corinth about A.D. 58, just before he left to return to Jerusalem (Rom. 15:25 and Acts 20:3). On this occasion the book of Acts tells us that Paul hastened to be in Jerusalem for the *"Feast of Pentecost"* (Acts 20:16). It is obvious from reading Romans 8 that Pentecost is on Paul's mind in more than one way. Not only would this be the last time Paul would ever be in Jerusalem, but this revelation from the apostle Paul in Romans is *double confirmation* to the truths depicted before in I Corinthians 15:20 and 23 about a Pentecostal resurrection and ascension of the Church of Jesus Christ.

It is evident from this passage of divine revelation that just as Christ was risen from the dead by the Holy Spirit of God, so the believer in Christ will be raised from the dead *by the same Spirit of God*. The resurrection of Christ and the resurrection of the believer are *vitally connected*. Christ's resurrection by the Spirit of God is the *guarantee* of the believer's resurrection. In fact, the text says that the same Spirit Who raised Christ from the dead dwells in the believer. In Christ's resurrection, He served as the *"Firstfruits"* sample and guarantee of the greater **"Firstfruits"** Harvest to come. The Holy Spirit, Who dwells in all believers, has *transfered* the Firstfruits *guarantee* from Christ **to all believers**. The believers, therefore, will benefit from the full blessings in the great *Firstfruits Harvest* resurrection of the Church of Jesus Christ. Thus, by the agency of the Holy Spirit of God, all believers constitute the **Harvest of Firstfruits,** awaiting the redemption of their bodies—i.e., the Rapture! Christ is represented by the *"Wave-sheaf Offering of Firstfruits"* at the time of Passover and the Church is thereby represented by the **"Wave-loaves of bread"** at the **"Harvest of Firstfruits"** celebrated 50 days later at Pentecost.

It is vital to remember that the special Offering of an early sample of grain during the Feast of Unleavened Bread (Passover) bears the same designation or name *Firstfruits,* as the *Feast of Firstfruits* which follows fifty days later (see Exo. 23:16; 34:22; Lev.23:17 and Num. 28:26). The special early Offering of the *Omer or Sheaf of Firstfruits* was the **token guarantee** of the full spring *Harvest of Firstfruits*. Thus, I repeat again, the resurrection and ascension of Christ is typified by the *Offering of the Omer* (or Sheaf) *of Firstfruits*. Likewise, the resurrection and ascension of the Church is typified by the *New Grain Offering* (the two Wave-loaves of bread) at the *Feast of Weeks* or *Feast of Firstfruits,* commonly called Pentecost.

As I stated in the beginning, the essential purpose of Pentecost served as a Harvest Feast celebration. As a Harvest Feast celebration, it is actually looking forward to the Harvest of its constituents—that is, of the field of grain at that particular season of the year. Paul was saying in these passages that the Church of Jesus Christ is that new *grain field*, and our resurrection (Rapture) is the harvest event as typified by the Feast of Pentecost.

Third,
Romans 15:15 and 16

"The OFFERING UP OF THE GENTILES"

Neverthless, brethren, I have written more boldly to you on some points, as reminding you, because of the grace given to me by God, that I might be *a minister* [lit., a serving priest] of Jesus Christ to the Gentiles, *ministering* [lit., in priestly service] the gospel of God, that the *offering* [as in the New Grain Offering] of the Gentiles might be acceptable, sanctified by the *Holy Spirit* [as with the anointing oil in the meal offerings]. (Rom. 15:15, 16—NKJV.)

. . . to be a minister of Christ Jesus to the Gentiles, ministering as a priest the gospel of God, that my offering of the Gentiles might become acceptable, sanctified by the Holy Spirit. (Rom. 15:16—NASB.)

In this beautiful passage of Scripture, the apostle Paul was inspired to describe his divine commission in terms of another figure or type—that of a *serving priest* in the Temple making or *ministering* an offering. In the translation from the Greek by the word simply as "minister," the significance can be missed. In this passage the word used for "minister" is that of a *"serving priest"* (*leittourgos*, or a public servant). Again, our usual English translation of "ministering" does not pick up the significance of what Paul is saying. Literally, the word for *"priestly service"* (*hierouggin*) is also used. The word for *"offering"* (literally, *prosphora* [*pros*, "to" and *phero*, "to bring"]) is used. It has reference to an offering such as would be presented to God in the Temple services. (See *W.E. Vine, Expository Dictionary of New Testament Words*, under "offering".)

In this case, the apostle Paul is speaking of himself as if he was ministering in a priestly duty of making an offering of the *Gentiles* to be acceptable to God by the Holy Spirit. Therefore, because of the unusual nature of this offering, being what is commonly considered unclean (Gentiles), it must be made *"acceptable"* and *"sanctified"* by the Holy Spirit—like oil mingled in the "grain offering" (Lev. 2:1). This whole description is actually a beautiful picture of the final offering up of the Gentiles to God in heaven at the end of this Age, much like that of the *"New Grain Offering"* in the form of two loaves of bread on that final (50th) Day of Pentecost.

So here we have what amounts to another reference to the Rapture of the Church, spelled out for us by the apostle Paul in terms of an **"OFFERING"** to God by means of the "priestly service" of Paul, himself. Consequently, no one should be the least disturbed by the fact that the Pentecostal Offering is, indeed, a type of the Rapture of the Church at a future designated and appointed time!

That future *time*, the antitypical 50th, is itself a complement to this particular Offering. The celebration of Pentecost is designated by the meaning of 50, which is *"fullness* or *completion."* Acts 2:1 is sometimes translated—"When the day of Pentecost had *fully* come, . . ." So this 50th Day actually prefigures ". . . until the *fullness* of the Gentiles has come in" as spoken of in Romans 11:25.

Paul, himself, has told us in the earlier passage of Romans 11:25 that the present blindness of the people of Israel will be lifted when "the *fullness* of the Gentiles has come in" (Rom. 11:25). The "fullness of the Gentiles" marks the completion of the Age of Grace and/or the Pentecostal Rapture of the Church.

Further Confirmations from Paul

There are actually many other Scriptures from the epistles of Paul which also demonstrate the vital connection between Christ's resurrection and the collective resurrection of the body of Christ, the Church. These references have the effect of *emphasizing* the blessed truth of Pentecost being prophetic of the Rapture. Note each passage carefully—

> *And if Christ is not risen,* your faith is futile; you are still in your sins! Then also those who have *fallen asleep in Christ have perished.* (1 Cor. 15:17, 18)

> That I may know Him and *the power of His resurrection,* and the fellowship of His sufferings, being conformed to His death, if, by any means, *I may attain to the resurrection from the dead.* (Philip. 3:10, 11)

> I press toward the goal for the prize of the *upward call* of God *in Christ Jesus.* (Philip. 3:14)

> For our citizenship is in heaven, from which we also eagerly wait for the Savior, the Lord Jesus Christ, Who will *transform our lowly body* that it may be *conformed to His glorious body,* . . . (Philip. 3:20, 21)

> Now He Who establishes us with you in Christ and has anointed us is God, Who also has sealed us and given us the Spirit in our hearts as *a guarantee.* (2 Cor. 1:21, 22)

> For we who are in this tent groan, being burdened, not because we want to be unclothed, but further clothed, that mortality may be swallowed up by life. Now He Who has prepared us for this very thing is God, Who also has given us the Spirit as a *guarantee.* (2 Cor. 5:5)

> In Him you also trusted, after you heard the word of truth, the gospel of your salvation; in Whom also having believed, you were sealed with the Holy Spirit of promise, *Who is the guarantee* of our inheritance until the *redemption of the purchased possession,*

> [i.e., the resurrection of the body] to the praise of His glory. (Eph. 1:13, 14)

> For if we believe that *Jesus died* and *rose again, in like manner* [lit. trans.] God *will bring with Him* [in resurrection] *those who sleep in Jesus.* (1 Thess. 4:14)

> To them God willed to make known what are the riches of the glory of this mystery among the Gentiles: which is *Christ **in you**, the hope of glory.* (Col. 1:27)

This last passage from Colossians is similar to saying, "since the Firstfruits guarantee is ***in us***, therefore, we have the great anticipation represented by the Pentecostal Feast of Firstfruits, i.e., the anticipation of THE HARVEST."

Another added ingredient which Moses gave to the observance of the two Harvest Feasts, Pentecost and Tabernacles, was the command for ***"rejoicing"*** (see Deut. 16:9–14). The Jews received notoriety for their execution of this command. No doubt, the apostle Paul alludes to this fact when he expresses the supreme joy of the saints being Raptured into the presence of the Lord.

> Then you shall keep the Feast of Weeks to the Lord . . . . You shall *rejoice* before the Lord your God, . . . [Deut. 16:10, 11].

> For what is our hope, or joy, or crown of ***rejoicing?*** *Is it not even you in the presence of our Lord Jesus Christ at His coming?* [1 Thess. 2:19].

Chapter Eight

FULL PURPOSE OF PENTECOST

I answered the question as to the purpose of Pentecost in a preliminary manner in the very first chapter. Pentecost, in its simplicity, was a harvest festival to celebrate the first harvest of the year. That was the only thing stated about it in the Law of Moses. The time designated by God for its celebration was likewise simply a time period which symbolizes "fullness or completion." In addition, it also became evident—when one reads the close of the four Gospel accounts and the first chapter of the book of Acts—that Christ was, as it were, planting a new field of grain beginning on the Day of Pentecost. This new field would come to be primarily composed of Gentile people.

In the Law of Moses there was nothing in the instructions concerning Pentecost to connect it with anything in Israel's early historic beginning as was done with the two major Feasts, one on each side of it. The earlier Feast of Passover was connected with the Passover deliverance of Israel out of Egyptian bondage. The later Feast of Tabernacles was connected to Israel's 40 year wandering in the wilderness and dwelling in booths. This actual, biblical disconnection of Pentecost from Israel's historic beginning has long been observed by Jewish teachers. This was compensated for by the tradition of the Pharisees who connected Pentecost with the giving of the Law from Mount Sinai some 50 days after the first Passover in Egypt. All readers of the biblical text admit this is not the stated purpose or designation revealed in the Scriptures for this Feast. It is true, however, by apparent coincidence that the Law program would immediately be revealed following that 50th day after Passover.

Actually, the only historic connection of this celebration, which we could say was scripturally indicated, came later in the early years of the time of the Judges who governed Israel. Even though the Feast is not specifically mentioned in the book of Ruth, yet the whole story of the redemption of a Gentile, who came to trust in Israel's Savior, takes place in the setting of this first harvest season. In fact, the story involves "the beginning of barley harvest" (Ruth 1:22), which was the time of the Offering of the Wave-sheaf, and continues to reach its climax at the "end . . . of the wheat harvest" (Ruth 2:23), which is the time of the Offering of the Wave-loaves. Consequently, all the Jewish people themselves recognize this connection and are, therefore, encouraged to read the book of Ruth at the time of the celebration of this Feast. We also saw that Jewish teachers have recognized that the story of Ruth takes place when a family of Israelites was displaced from their land, much like the "Diaspora" of the Jews during the last two thousand years. In that setting, the redemption of this Gentile occurs just at the time of the spring harvest season in Israel. Herein is the scriptural clue for another deeper purpose for Pentecost. Pentecost, therefore, has the theme of Gentile redemption vitally connected to its observance at the very time of Israel's dispersion.

Now we can answer the question—

Why Was The Church Born On Pentecost?

We can now answer that question by the fact, according to the New Testament, that the Church, as a *new grain field*, was born upon the Day of Pentecost which came to be primarily characterized by the salvation of Gentile believers. In other words, as was true in the book of Ruth, this is a season and a Day that came to have special meaning for the Gentile believers. Thus we have the Pentecostal connection to both Israel, at a time of its *faithlessness*, and to the "out-calling" of Gentiles, at a time of their *faithfulness*. The Gentiles then came to worship the God of Israel in thankfulness and in great anticipation.

The fact that the Church of Jesus Christ was born on that Day, and at the precise hour of the special Wave-loaves Offering, clearly points to Pentecost as a type of the Church. It was the Church's Day. Even those who say Pentecost only typified the coming of the Holy Spirit must admit that the Holy Spirit of Pentecost "baptizes" all believers "into one body . . . the Church which is Christ's body" (Acts 1:4, 5 and 1 Cor. 12:13). Therefore, they are saying, in effect, *the very same thing*!

(1) The particular *Offering* on that Day very obviously symbolizes the Church! The "New Grain Offering" (Lev. 23:16) represents the "One New Man," or the "New Creation" in Christ (Eph. 2:15 and 2 Cor. 5:17). The "bread" of the Offering represents the Church as the "One Bread" of I Corinthians 10:17.

(2) The special story highlighted in the book of Ruth is how she came to "*find grace*" in the eyes of a kinsman-redeemer (Ruth 2:2 and 10). The special description of this present age of Gentile salvation is "the Dispensation of *the Grace* of God" (Eph. 3:2 and John 1:17; Acts 20:24, Rom. 5:2).

(3) Both Jewish teachers and Christian teachers have fully recognized the special association in the book of Ruth of the story of *Gentile conversion* to be associated with the time and event of the Firstfruit Harvest season in Israel. Of course, the present Dispensation of Grace is likewise the time of the special "out-calling of *the Gentile people*" for Christ's name (Acts 15:14 and Rom. 11:25).

(4) We saw in chapter four certain dispensational implications demonstrated by the Feast of Pentecost. The Pentecostal arrangement in the year actually foreshadowed dispensational characteristics of this Church Age. (a) The Feast was *parenthetical* between Passover and Tabernacles, and so is the Church situated between the Law and the Kingdom Ages. (b) The Feast was described as a "*mystery*," and so was the Church Age. (c) Pentecost was not connected to any *historical event of Israel's early history* as are the other two Feasts; neither is the Rapture of the Church. (d) Pentecost

came to be associated with *the theme of Gentile salvation* in the book of Ruth, as in this present Age. (e) Pentecost is to be celebrated on the 50th day which symbolizes "*fullness or completion,*" and the Church is to be Raptured when "the fullness of the Gentiles comes in." (f) Some 50 days after Passover *the Law was instituted* in Sinai; at the completion of the antitypical 50 days (i.e., the Rapture), the Law will be reinstituted. (g) Under the Civil Calendar of Israel, Pentecost is the *last Feast* to be observed before the New Year; after the Rapture of the Church, Israel's Age of Law will resume. (h) Pentecost is *missing in the Kingdom celebrations,* which implies that its total fulfillment has been accomplished. (i) The short and abrupt nature of Pentecost, unlike the other week long celebrations, typically infers the abrupt Rapture. (j) It is the only Feast that does not have a specified monthly calendar date for its observance—nor is there a calendar date for the Rapture of the Church.

(5) And finally, what I am emphasizing in this book is that the special Offering on this Feast day is designed to draw our attention to Pentecost as one primary *prophecy* of the Rapture of the Church! Surprisingly enough, almost all pretribulational Rapture expositors have missed this very clear and simple testimony. However, it should now be obvious to us, that if the waving up in the air of the sheaf of "Firstfruits" at Passover was a type of the **resurrection and ascension of Christ**, then, to be consistent, the waving up in the air of the "New Grain Offering" is equally typical of **the resurrection and ascension of the Church of Jesus Christ**. The first Offering is the basis for interpreting the second. As the first Offering of "Firstfruit" saw its final fulfillment at the climactic resurrection and ascension of Christ, so the second Offering must see its final climactic fulfillment *at the resurrection and ascension of the Church*. In consistency with this, the apostle Paul has now directly applied the typology of the Feast *to the Rapture of the Church* in these several Scriptures which we have read in the previous chapter.

(6) As if in confirmation of this truth, we shall shortly see that the Holy Spirit of inspiration applies the Greek word *harpazo*, meaning "caught up" or "raptured," to both events—that of Christ's resurrection and ascension, and that of the Church's resurrection and ascension. In addition, Paul said—

"If the *Firstfruit* is Holy, the *Lump* is also Holy"

The fundamental principle that the apostle Paul stated in Romans 11:16 must apply. *"For if the Firstfruit* [Christ] *is holy, the Lump* [the Church] *is also holy."* What is true of the "Firstfruit," as a sample, must be true of the whole "batch of dough." The word *"lump"* (Greek, *phurama*), "denotes that which is mixed or kneaded, hence a mass of dough" (W.E. Vine). This principle which Paul stated is perfectly illustrated in the subject before us. In Leviticus 23:10 and 11 we see the order for waving the Sheaf of Firstfruit. Immediately following, in verses 16 and 17, we see the order for making the mass of dough into two loaves of bread and waving them before the Lord as well. What is true of the *Firstfruit* (Christ) is also true of the *two loaves of Bread* (the Church). Many Scriptures attest to the fact that the Church's resurrection and Rapture is vitally connected to, and dependent upon, the "Firstfruit" sample of Jesus Christ.

If this "New Grain Offering," of two loaves of bread waved in the air at Pentecost, is NOT a type of the resurrection and ascension of the Church, then neither is the earlier "Sheaf of Firstfruits" waved in the air at Passover a type of the resurrection and ascension of Jesus Christ! However, if Christ's resurrection and ascension is typified by the "Sheaf of Firstfruits" waved at Passover—*and the Holy Spirit says it is*—then, of course, the Church's resurrection and ascension must be typified by the "New Grain Offering" waved at Pentecost! This sound conclusion is inescapable!

In addition, in the previous chapter I quoted from several major commentaries on these two Offerings. All of them make the very same observation. The symbolism of resurrection in the first Offering demands the symbolism of resurrection in the second Offering. So this is not some outlandish conclusion. I say again, this sound conclusion is positively inescapable because of the very example of our Lord Jesus Christ, Himself!

Three Areas of Example

As I stated in my introductory remarks, many years ago I began a study of the apparent incongruity of Christ being crucified on the traditional "Good Friday" in Christendom, *which is the day after the sacrifice of the Passover lambs*, with the fact that this does not coincide with the Passover typology, nor with certain statements in the Gospel accounts. In the process of time, I discovered that this tradition of Christendom was due to pagan contamination and theological confusion as to what the inspired writers of the Greek Scriptures were saying. To my happy surprise, I found crystal clear proof that there is perfect harmony between the type and the antitype. For proof of this see my book, *The Day Christ Died as Our Passover.* Just here I will use this event as an example of what is also true about the typology in the Feast of Pentecost.

Notice how each ingredient in the Passover celebration as to its Days and Offering has *three* specific areas of typical fulfillment: (1) *the substance or ingredients* in the offering, (2) *the action* of the offering, and (3) *the timing* of the offering.

I. The biblical record reveals that (1) **unblemished lambs** were to be (2) **chosen and selected** on (3) **the 10th day of Nisan** as the Passover lambs to later be sacrificed.

In perfect Fulfillment—

Our Lord Jesus Christ was the (1) **unblemished Lamb** (2) **chosen and selected** on (3) **the 10th day of Nisan** (A.D. 30, according to most biblical historians today) to be the antitypical Passover Lamb for the salvation of the world (John 1:29 and 12:27, 32). For four days He was examined and remained spotless and impeccable.

(1) The <u>Substance</u>—*the lambs*   Christ as *The Lamb of God*.
(2) The <u>Action</u> of *choosing*   Christ, *Chosen by the multitude*.
(3) The <u>time</u>—*10th of Nisan*   On Schedule—*10th of Nisan*.

II. The biblical record further shows clearly that (1) **the Passover lamb** as a perfect type of Christ in His redemptive work for mankind (2) **was sacrificed** on (3) **the afternoon of the 14th Day of Nisan.**

In Perfect Fulfillment—

"*Christ our* (1) ***Passover*** [Lamb] *was* (2) ***sacrificed for us***" (I Cor. 5:7) on (3) **the 14th Day of Nisan** (A.D. 30). Everything in this area of typology was fulfilled to perfection.

(1) The <u>Substance</u>—*the lamb*   Christ as *The Lamb of God.*
(2) The <u>Action</u>—*sacrificed*   *sacrificed for us.*
(3) The <u>Time</u>—*afternoon, 14th*   Precisely *on Schedule, afternoon of the 14th*

III. The biblical record shows clearly that (1) the **bundle of grain** offering (the "Firstfruits") was (2) **waved up in the air** (3) on **the morning after the regular Sabbath** which occurs during this Feast. This was another type of Christ.

Fulfilled to Perfection—

The Scripture says (1) "**Christ the Firstfruits**" (1 Cor. 15:23) was (2) **resurrected and ascended** (3) on **Sunday morning** exactly on schedule. This typology was fulfilled to perfection in Christ's glorious resurrection from the dead, and His first early ascension to the Father at that same time.

(1) The <u>Ingredients</u>—*grain*   Christ *The Firstfruits*.
(2) The <u>Action</u>—*waved up*   Christ *Resurrected and Ascended*.
(3) The <u>Time</u>—*Sunday A.M.*   Precisely *on Schedule, Sunday A.M.*

Now let us look at a fourth example—

On Pentecost of A.D. 30, A Preliminary Fourth Example

IV. The biblical record shows clearly that the Feast of Pentecost is a type of the Church in its resurrection and ascension—i.e., the Rapture (Rom. 8:11, 23; 15:15, 16 and I Cor. 15:23, etc.). This aspect of the typology remains to be fulfilled at the Rapture of the Church. (1) **The New Grain Offering** (two loaves of bread) (2) **waved up in the air** (3) on Sunday A.M., **50 days** after the Passover "Wave-sheaf Offering."

Shall be Fulfilled when—

(1) The **"New Man"** being **"one bread"** (typical of the Church) (2) is to be **resurrected and ascended** (3) when **"the fullness [50th] of the Gentiles has come in"** (Rom. 11:23).

(1) The Ingredients— *bread*	The Church, the *"bread"*
(2) The Action—*waved up*	*Resurrection and Rapture*
(3) The Time—*50th day*	To be Precisely *on Schedule* (50th), at the completion of this Age, when the "fullness of the Gentiles comes in."

When one looks *by faith* at the breathtaking precision of God's calendar and its fulfillment thus far, we can only pray that our lives will be fully dedicated to God's will for us. God's appointed time for the Church to be resurrected, ascended and presented in the heavens, no doubt, draws increasingly near. At the *"completion"* (50th, Pentecost) of the out-calling of the Gentiles, the Rapture will take place. Pentecost, therefore, not only marks the *birth* of the Church but, more precisely, its *Rapture* into heaven as well. Once it all happens, no doubt, we will all look back and wonder how it was that we so easily often forgot, during the business and problems of our earthly sojourn, the beautiful and guaranteed promises of God.

Both Christ and the Church "Raptured"

For anyone who would still doubt that the resurrection and ascension of Christ could ever be equated with or be a precursor to the Rapture of the Church, please take note of the amazing fact which the Spirit of God reveals in the book of Revelation. In Revelation 12:5 Christ is depicted by the apostle John as the "Child Who was to rule all nations" being "CAUGHT UP to God and His throne." Now the words "caught up" here are from the Greek word *harpazo*, which is the identical word used of the Rapture of the Church by Paul in 1 Thessalonians 4:17, ". . . shall be CAUGHT UP [*harpazo*] together with them in the clouds to meet the Lord in the air." So it is a scriptural fact that what is stated of the One (Christ our Lord) is also stated of the other (the Church which is His body). We can now understand that as Christ was "caught up" or *Raptured* into heaven, so it is that the "Church which is Christ's body" will also be "caught up" or *Raptured* into heaven. It becomes a fitting reality that what happens to the "Head of the body" also happens to "the body," (i.e., the Church) itself.

Note the following chart which illustrates this reality.

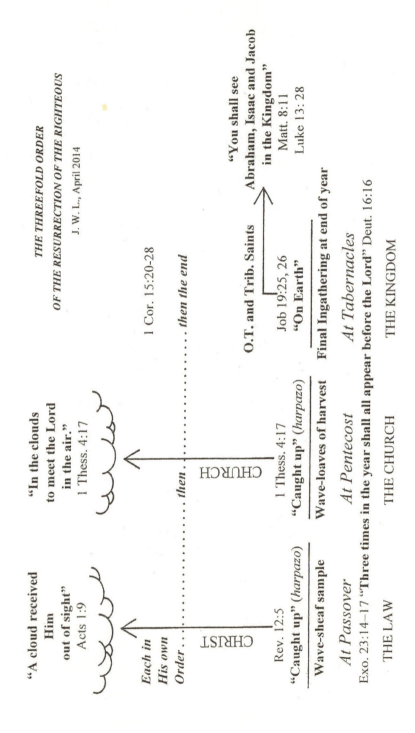

Chapter Nine
ENOCH and PENTECOST

The Translation of Enoch

I did not mention Enoch when I wrote the earlier chapter on typologies. This was partly due to the fact that there is a great deal of mystery surrounding this person. It was also due to the fact that what is known about Enoch is certainly vitally apropos to this Rapture subject and I wanted to save discussing it till now. One certain thing is the unusual fact that his story is so brief and yet the amount of information is so large. Most certainly, the Jewish sages and rabbis did a lot of thinking about this man. From the very first few centuries since the birth of the Church, Christians have also seen beautiful truths in Enoch. The similarity between Enoch being "translated" (as stated in the King James Version of Heb. 11:5) and the revelation given to the apostle Paul of the translation or "Rapture" of the Church of Jesus Christ is too obvious for anyone to miss.

The whole Hebrew text concerning Enoch in Genesis 5 bears repeating—

> Enoch lived sixty-five years, and became the father of Methuselah. Then Enoch walked with God three hundred years after he became the father of Methuselah, and he had other sons and daughters. So all the days of Enoch were three hundred and sixty-five years. Enoch walked with God; and he was not, for God took him. (Gen. 5:21–24, NASB.)

The writer of the book of Hebrews states—

> By faith Enoch was taken up so that he would not see death; 'And he was not found because God took him up'; for he obtained the witness that before his being taken up he was pleasing to God. (Heb. 11:5, NASB.)

Any believer who rejoices in the truth about the Rapture of the Church can't help but also be extremely curious about this man, Enoch. And, indeed, many Bible teachers have indicated that Enoch can be viewed as a type of the Rapture of the Church. Some of the interesting basic similarities I have gathered are the following list.

Enoch and the Rapture

(1) Both Enoch and the last generation of the Church are said to be leaving this earth **without dying**. In Enoch's case, he was simply taken by God and, as stated in Hebrews, he did *"not see death."* As to the Church of Jesus Christ, *"we shall not all sleep* [see death]." All those who are still alive at the coming of the Lord "will be caught up" with the resurrected dead to "meet the Lord in the air" (1 Thess. 4:17 and 1 Cor. 15:51, 52). The very thought of multiplied millions being "taken" without seeing death is really beyond our comprehension.

(2) Notice in both cases that they simply do not only disappear, but they are *"**taken up**"* or *"**caught up**"* out of this world system, by God's very presence, into heaven. This means that in both cases the Lord directly takes them.

(3) The sudden disappearance of Enoch and of the living Church saints would also mean that the remaining earthlings could not find them. This is indicated in the Genesis statement *"he* [Enoch] *was not"*; the writer to the Hebrews expressed that *"**he was not found**."* Of course, when the Church disappears, I don't think our imaginations can begin to tell us what chaos is going to happen because, in this case, we are talking about the sudden disappearance of multiplied millions of people from all over this globe. There is no question that many—probably relatives, neighbors

and business acquaintances—will be looking and searching for these missing people, but they will "*not be found.*"

(4) *The Hastings Dictionary of the Bible* makes the statement: "'Enoch walked with God, and was not, for God took him.' The idea here is suggested that, because of his perfect fellowship with God, this patriarch was 'translated' to heaven without tasting death." This observation seems to be true. The writer of Hebrews states, "he [Enoch] was **pleasing to God**." Now, when I look out at Christendom today, my first thought is, "there is no way believers in this time of the Church's defection and apostasy could be characterized by walking like Enoch!" But then, on the other hand, as I remember the truth of Paul's revelation about *God's manifold grace* to us in this age, I realize that the only reason God is going to Rapture up the Church is precisely because of the **Perfectly Righteous Man** Who is within us—Jesus Christ. And, indeed, this is exactly how our translation is stated by Paul—"CHRIST IN YOU, the hope of glory" (Col. 1:27). Yes, the only reason we are "going up" is because of the One Whom God sees in us! In 1 Corinthians 1:29–31 Paul states, ". . . that no flesh should glory in His presence. But of Him you are in Christ Jesus, Who became for us wisdom from God—and *righteousness* and *sanctification* and *redemption*—that, as it is written, 'He who glories, let him glory in the Lord.'" So, if Enoch was taken up because of his righteousness, then the Church of Jesus Christ is going to be taken up *ONLY* because of Christ's perfect righteousness credited to every believer. And indeed, that must be the case because this is the age of the revelation of God's multiplied graces to believers, who are viewed by God as standing in His Divine Son of perfect righteousness—"IN HIM [Christ, Jesus] we have obtained an inheritance, . . ." (Eph. 1:11).

Just think of it! Now we know *why* the Rapture! Precisely ". . . to the intent that now the manifold wisdom of God might be made known by [or through] the Church to the principalities and powers in the heavenly places, according to the eternal purpose which He *accomplished in Christ Jesus our Lord*" (Eph. 3:10 and 11).

(5) And who was Enoch in relationship to the human family? We couldn't say he was a Jew or a Gentile because those divisions of the human family had not yet occurred. On the other hand, we can look at Enoch as a member of the **new human family** (in Adam) which God had recently created a few chapters earlier. And that is precisely what the Scriptures say about the members of the Church. "For in Christ Jesus neither circumcision [a Jew] nor uncircumcision [a Gentile] avails anything, but a **new creation**" (Gal.6:15). And it is important to remember that this "new creation" is vitally connected to our Savior Who is designated as "the last Adam" (1 Cor. 15:45). As a result of our being connected to "the second Man" (1 Cor. 15:47) we have the guarantee—"even so in Christ shall all be made alive" (1 Cor. 15:22).

(6) And just when did Enoch live? In Jude 14 we are reminded that Enoch "was the *Seventh* from Adam." Isn't that interesting! Here we have the "**number of completion**" (7) in association with the one who was "taken up." As this would relate to the Church, we have seen before that it was born on the 50th day. This is understood to be the number of "God's perfect completion [1 + seven times seven]." In addition, the Church will also be Raptured at the number of God's perfect completion.

Enoch and Prophecy

(7) And what is Enoch's relation to the Judgment which was to come upon the earth? If one were to tabulate the years in the chronology, Enoch was "taken up" over 650 years before the Great Flood. However, if one were to simply observe the brevity of the account, then Enoch would be seen as only eight verses away from Noah and the great calamity. Therefore, it has been pointed out that Enoch was "translated" **before the judgment of the flood**, representing the Church being taken before the Great Tribulation—whereas, Noah and his family were preserved through the flood, representing a remnant of Israel being preserved through the Great Tribulation to enter the Kingdom.

(8) In Jude 14 and 15 we are told that Enoch prophesied concerning the ungodly persecutors and blasphemers of God's truth and of the saints—

> Now Enoch, the seventh from Adam, prophesied about these men also, saying, 'Behold the Lord comes with ten thousands of His saints [holy ones], to execute judgment on all, to convict all who are ungodly among them of all their ungodly deeds which they have committed in an ungodly way, and of all the harsh things which ungodly sinners have spoken against Him.'

Of course, the "steward" of this "mystery" age (Col. 1:25–27, Eph. 3:2) and "the Apostle to the Gentiles," Paul, made the very same prophecy. See 2 Thessalonians 1:7–9,

> ... rest with us when the Lord Jesus is revealed from heaven with His mighty angels, in flaming fire taking vengeance on those who do not know God, and upon those who do not obey the gospel of our Lord Jesus Christ. These shall be punished with everlasting destruction from the presence of the Lord and from the glory of His power, ...

Enoch and the Mysteries

(9) I said before that there is a lot of "mystery" surrounding Enoch. The small amount which is told about him in the Genesis account, and yet the magnitude of what God did with him, leave our minds with a lot of questions. The Jews, themselves, focused upon this aspect of Enoch. *The Pentateuch & Haftorahs, Second Edition*, edited by the Chief Rabbi of the British Empire, London, 1972, in commentary on Enoch said,

> Rabbinical legend was very busy with the story of Enoch. He was the repository of the *mysteries* of the

universe; and even higher honors were later accorded to him in the circles of Jewish mystics. (Bold italics mine, J. L.)

Of course, the Church itself was also a repository of the "mysteries" of God for this age—". . . the *mystery* which has been hidden from ages and from generations, but now has been revealed to His saints. To them God willed to make known what are the riches of the glory of this *mystery* among the Gentiles: which is Christ in you, the hope of glory" (Col. 1:26, 27).

(10) In the *Encyclopaedia Judaica*, 1971, Vol. 6, page 794, concerning Enoch it is stated that "In the Aggadah [the amplification of the Jewish Law and history] . . . [Enoch] was the guardian of the **secret of intercalation**." This has reference to one who has the ability to make the calendar year correspond to the solar year. This is stated of Enoch because he is said to live "365 years," which is also the exact number of days in a year.

As to the present Age of Grace, it indeed was a "secret" (Eph. 3:1–6), and most assuredly, it will be completed in exact harmony with God's heavenly solar system of operations (Eph. 1:10 and Rom. 11:25).

(11) In the same article from the Aggadah concerning Enoch, it is stated, "Enoch lived in a secret place as a hidden righteous man and was **called by an angel** to leave his retreat to go **to teach men** to walk in the ways of God."

I do not doubt that Enoch was a preacher of righteousness, but it must have been like Noah, who was an "heir of the righteousness which is by faith" (Heb. 11:7). Most certainly, the Church of Jesus Christ has been called to "go into all the world" (Matt. 28:19) and teach the gospel of the grace of God. We can tell the world of the free gift of "the righteousness which is by faith in Christ Jesus" (Rom. 3:21, 22).

(12) Again, in the same article from the Jewish Aggadah, God is reported to have explained to the angels why Enoch was taken up into heaven: "Be not offended, for all mankind denied Me and My dominion and paid homage to idols; I therefore transferred the **Shekhinah** [*'Divine Presence'*] **from earth to heaven**, and this man Enoch is the *elect* of men." So it is thought, by the transfer of the *Shekhinah*, that Enoch was transferred with Him into heaven. Apparently the Jewish thinkers associated Enoch's being "taken up" from this earth with the Shekhinah Glory being "taken up" from the Temple and the earth—as described in Ezekiel chapter 10—because of Israel's very own idolatry and apostasy.

Now this is an amazing statement from the Aggadah—in light of the fact that it is the *Holy Spirit* of God, the *"Shekhinah Presence"* today, Who "dwells in us" (Rom. 8:9). And, furthermore, it is stated "But if the Spirit of Him Who raised Jesus from the dead *dwells in you*, He Who raised Christ from the dead will also give life to your mortal bodies *through His Spirit Who dwells in you*" (Rom. 8:11). In addition, in 2 Thessalonians 2:7 we are told of the Spirit, "He Who now restrains will do so until *He is taken out of the midst*." So it is revealed that the Church will be transferred by, and in association with, the "Shekhinah Presence." In addition, I should not leave out the fact that the Church constitutes "the *elect* of God" today (Rom. 8:33; Col. 3:12 and Titus 1:1).

Enoch and Pentecost

(13) In the *Legends of the Jews*, by Lewis Ginsberg, it is stated concerning him, "The Translation of Enoch.... Enoch was born on the sixth day of the month Sivan, and he was taken to heaven in the same month, Sivan, on the same day and in the same hour when he was born." Now the sixth day of Sivan, according to Jewish tradition, is the **Day of Pentecost**. And they are herein saying that Enoch was both born on that very day and also that he ascended into heaven on that very same day and hour. Amazing!

Of course, this just so happens to be one main thesis in this study—that the Scriptures reveal that the Day of Pentecost is not only the birthday of the Church of Jesus Christ, but it is also prophetic of the very termination day of the Church's existence on earth, i.e., the Rapture of the Church. I do not know why the Jews thought of this, other than the fact that they considered both Enoch and the Feast of Shavuot to be associated with "mysteries." But I most certainly do know why I am scripturally contending for that reality concerning the relationship between Pentecost and the Rapture!

(14) It is also a well-known fact that a second and third century strong Jewish opposition to the Enoch account in Genesis arose in Judaism, primarily because of the Christian usage of this story. Such is indicated in both the *Encyclopaedia Judaica* and the *Pentateuch & Haftorahs*. The *Encyclopaedia Judaica* states under *the Aggadah:*

> The third-century Palestinian rabbis deny the miraculous translation of Enoch, and state that he vacillated all his life between righteousness and sinfulness, whereupon God removed him from the world before he relapsed again into sin (Gen. R. 25:1). This derogatory evaluation of Enoch was, at least in part, a reaction against the use made by Christians of the legend of Enoch's ascension to heaven.

This was a sad reaction by certain Jews of the second and third centuries. Today the Jewish people do not seem to carry this same animosity towards the story of Enoch, nor have they manufactured these same slanderous remarks. In response to this, I would now affirm and pray that, when the Rapture of the Church phenomena does occur before their very eyes, the Jewish people will relate to this by the reality of the story of Enoch which is found in their very own Scriptures. Not only is there a clear parallel between the "taking up" of Enoch and the "catching away" of the Church, but the Rapture event is also prefigured in the Feast of Pentecost. I hope many of the Jewish people will also come to realize this beautiful truth as well.

Some people love a "mystery story." And indeed, to the world this will be the "mystery of all mysteries." The Rapture of the Church will occur on the day prefigured by Pentecost, which simply means "fullness or completion"—in this case, "the fullness of the Gentiles."

Chapter Ten

THE APPROACHING PENTECOST

A Unique Feature of Passover

At the beginning of this study I stated that it is an important fact to note that the Feast of Passover stands as a marker for both the *beginning* and the *close* of the Law Dispensation. It is very important to observe that this arrangement was not an accident of happenstance. With the first Passover in Egypt, Israel, as a nation, congregation or church, was called out of Egypt to serve God in the wilderness. This was when Israel was *born* as a nation. This was also when the Dispensation of the Law actually began. The very day (the 15th of Abib) that the children of Israel left Egypt marked the termination of the 430 years since the Promise was given to Abraham (Exodus 12:40, 41); therefore it also was the beginning of a new Age for the Israelites.

Jeremiah spoke concerning the Law Covenant, "... the Covenant that I [the LORD] made with their fathers *in the **day** that I took them by the hand to lead them out of the land of Egypt*, ..." (Jer. 31:32). This means that the celebration of Passover was the first of the ceremonial Law observances to be given. Therefore, we understand that the first Passover in Egypt marked the actual birth of the nation of Israel and the *beginning* of the Law Dispensation.

However, most realize that the Passover event was primarily *prophetic* in nature. It was to actually have its prime spiritual fulfillment in the death of Jesus Christ for the redemption of Israel and beyond her for the spiritual redemption of all mankind. This would happen when *"the fullness of time had come"* for the appearance of the antitypical Passover Lamb (Gal. 4:4). When this exact *"consummation of the ages"* took place, Christ *"appeared to put away sin by the sacrifice of Himself"* (Heb. 9:26). Thus the final Passover in Israel's history, which would formally mark the spiritual fulfillment of the Passover subject, took place in the last week of Christ's earthly ministry. Most historians now calculate this as taking place in A. D. 30. Christ's death also had the effect of the legal termination of the Mosaic Law Dispensation. This is when Israel's own rejected Messiah was sacrificed as the antitypical Passover Lamb. In the reckoning of God in heaven, this is when the Law was *"nailed to the cross"*—see Ephesians 2:14–16 and Colossians 2:14. Thus, Christ's Passover formally marked the (temporary) termination of the Law. This truth about the termination of the Law was gradually made known, primarily through the revelations given to the apostle Paul.

It should be explained that the history in the book of Acts actually records for us the formal transition of the early Church out of Judaism into pure Christianity. The first assembly of believers were all Jewish, who were faithfully practicing the Law, and were therefore considered during these early years as simply another sect of Judaism. Then, when the "door of faith" was opened to the Gentile people, of necessity, a modification of the Law for the allowance of the association of believing Jews with believing Gentiles was spiritually understood. At first the Jewish believers themselves would continue to practice the Law, whereas the Gentile believers were free from its obligations (Acts 15). By the time the book of Hebrews was written (at the end of the Acts period), the inspired writer could clearly say to the Hebrew saints—"Now what is *becoming obsolete and growing old* [i.e., the Law system under the First Covenant] *is ready to vanish away"* (Heb. 8:13). And, as if on schedule, the whole Temple complex was shortly thereafter totally destroyed in A. D. 70. The Church, therefore, experienced a 40 year transition out of Judaism into pure Christianity.

Time of the Rapture of the Church

According to all the Greek Scriptures, and certainly through the apostle Paul, we understand that the Feast of Pentecost marks both the ***beginning*** and the ***close*** of the Dispensation of the Grace of God. The Church was born on the Day of Pentecost in Jerusalem in A.D. 30. However, the Feast of Pentecost (like the Passover) is primarily *prophetic* in nature. But, we have asked in this study, what is Pentecost actually prophetic of ? Here is the failure which most expositors have made in times past. Since the Church was born on this Feast day, they have merely understood or assumed that the Feast was only prophetic of the birth of the Church or, as some would say, of the coming of the Holy Spirit. In reality, this is only the beginning of the story, but not its *prime feature*.

As we have seen in this study, the Feast of Pentecost can be viewed as typical of many things. By its unique parenthetical position on the calendar, it is actually prophetic of this whole present age, which is also parenthetical in nature. The first Pentecost in Acts also represents the beginning sowing or planting of a whole new field of grain. In addition, Pentecost, especially by the uniqueness of its Offering, is also prophetic of the resurrection and ascension of the Church as its harvest celebration. It is therefore true that the Feast bears ingredients which would symbolize some of the unique characteristics of the Church of Jesus Christ, and even of this Age of Grace. However, in this book I am pointing out that its prophetic perspective points towards the Rapture of that Church by the harvesting and waving up in the air of the two loaves of bread. Therefore, Pentecost will have its *total fulfillment* at the time of the Rapture of the Church of Jesus Christ. This is the part that most expositors have missed.

The totally fulfilled Pentecost will therefore, likewise, terminate the pilgrim journey of the Church of Jesus Christ on earth. And, no doubt, the Church will be Raptured *on God's schedule*. The only question that any believer should ask is, "When will the *antitypical* 50th day [*the fullness or completion*] occur?" Of course, we all must realize that the determination of that "fullness" rests in God's wisdom and timing alone. Very soon, we hope! When God decrees that the *"fullness* [or completion] of the Gentiles has come in" (Rom. 11:16 and 25), He will authorize the trumpet to sound, calling the Church of Jesus Christ to assemble. The voice of Christ will be heard and, as the "New Grain Offering," the Church will be presented up to God.

Great anticipation was generated when the Jewish households "counted the days" until the Feast of Shavuot. So it has also been true down through the centuries of this Church Age. Every generation of true believers has "counted the days," as it were, when they refreshed their hearts with the promises of God concerning the Rapture. It is not accidentally called "The Blessed Hope"—Titus 2:13 and Colossians 1:27.

The Passover which Closed the Age of Law

In going back to the Passover which closed the Age of Law, one must look at the prophecy of Daniel. There we are told that after 483 years had transpired, the Messiah would be "cut off" (Daniel 9:25, 26). This gave the people of Israel a certain year to look forward to in their expectations. Perhaps the most difficult thing about Daniel's prophecy was in understanding what it meant that the Messiah would be "cut off." Even the close disciples of Christ did not understand that their Messiah would first have to suffer and die.

Whatever "the sufferings of Christ" meant to the disciples, it seemed to be pushed aside in their thinking by the great crescendo of His popularity among the common people. The disciples had focused upon the *reign* of their Messiah and not on His *sufferings*. The two aspects seemed incompatible, if not contradictory, to them.

Actually, therefore, the Passover which would take place just after the conclusion of the 483rd year of Daniel's prophecy became most important as to the time the Kingdom would arrive. This was true for two reasons. First of all, that Passover would be associated with the conclusion of the 483 years in Daniel's prophecy simply because it would mark the beginning of a new year on Israel's liturgical calendar. In addition, as I stated at the beginning of this study, the prophets Isaiah and Jeremiah had predicted the establishment of the New Covenant and the deliverance of Israel in connection with a greater Passover celebration (Isa. 31:5; Jer. 23:7, 8 and 31:31–34).

Of course, not all the people fully understood these prophecies, especially in light of Israel's national rejection of her King. Certainly the rulers of Israel felt this anticipation, but at the same time they were vague or else blinded as to what would happen to the nation. Nevertheless, it is amazing that at the time of the final Passover when Christ was about to die, we are told that there was great excitement and expectancy in Israel that possibly the Messiah and Kingdom were about to appear—

> Now when He was asked by the Pharisees *when the Kingdom of God would come*, . . . (Luke 17:20)

> Now as they heard these things, He spoke another parable, because they thought *the Kingdom of God would appear immediately.* (Luke 19:11)

> Now behold, there was a man named Joseph, a council member, a good and just man. He had not consented to their decision and deed [against Christ]. He was from Arimathea, a city of the Jews, who himself was also *waiting for the Kingdom of God.* (Luke 23:50, 51)

No doubt, this expectation was due to the fact of Daniel's prophecy, and that of the other prophets who aligned Israel's Kingdom hopes with a future "passing over" by God in executing their deliverance from all nations on earth. And most certainly, it was because in the ministries of John the Baptist and Christ, Himself, there was the offer of this Kingdom; both affirmed that the "Kingdom of God was near at hand" (Matt. 3:2 and 4:17).

In addition, it is important to remember that on the night of Christ's last supper, which we understand was, in fact, the pre-Passover supper in custom at that time (and still is in Israel till this very day), Christ very plainly told the disciples that He would never again "eat of it [the Passover supper] until it is *fulfilled in the Kingdom of God.*" Here are His exact words—

> Then He said to them, 'With fervent desire I have desired to eat this Passover with you before I suffer; for I say to you, I will no longer eat of it *until it is fulfilled in the Kingdom of God.*' Then He took the cup, and gave thanks, and said, 'Take this and divide it among yourselves; for I will not drink of the fruit of the vine *until the Kingdom of God comes.* (Luke 22:15–18, italics mine, J. L.)

What Christ said here means that there was going to be a *gap in time*—from this observance of Passover by Christ just before His death—until there would come the future fulfillment of God's promises to Israel in the *Kingdom of God.* At that time Messiah will reign on earth in great majesty, having defeated all His enemies, and will sit down once again with His disciples and observe Passover. In other words, Christ is telling the disciples that there is going to be an unspecified *interval of time* between this "last supper" and the future establishment of the Kingdom of God.

Thus, the prophecy of Daniel can likewise be understood to indicate a similar gap in time between the event of the Messiah being "cut off" and the conclusion of that final week of prophesy. Let us read Daniel 9:24–26—

> Seventy weeks [of years] are determined for your people and for your holy city, . . . Know therefore and understand that from the going forth of the command to restore and build Jerusalem until the Messiah the Prince, there shall be seven weeks and sixty-two weeks; . . . And after the sixty- two weeks *Messiah shall be cut off*, but not for Himself; and the people of the prince who is to come *shall destroy the city and the sanctuary.* The end of it shall be with a flood, and till the end wars and desolations are determined. (Italics mine, J. L.)

So it was, because of the hardness of their hearts, the rulers of Israel rejected the King and the promised Kingdom. Therefore, this Passover of A.D. 30 would not mark the establishment of the Kingdom of God for Israel. Rather, it would mark the death of the Messiah as the antitypical Passover Lamb and the close of the Law Dispensation, for at this time the Law was "nailed to the cross." Christ had very soberly and sadly spoken of the fact that Israel, in the main, *"knew not the time of their visitation"* (See Luke 19:44), and they carnally could not *"discern the signs of the times"* (Matt. 16:3).

Obviously, the disciples did not know how long this gap of time would be. Therefore, the very first thing they asked the risen Christ just before His ascension was "Lord, will you *at this time* restore *the Kingdom to Israel?*" (Acts 1:6). To this Christ responded, "It is not for you to know the times or seasons which the Father has put in His own authority" (Acts 1:7). In other words, once again there would be an unspecified gap in time between Christ's first coming and His second to establish that Kingdom. And then, as the disciples started preaching the "good news," the Holy Spirit began revealing to them the broadness and grandeur of this "parenthetical" Age of Grace.

The Antitypical "Pentecost" which Closes the Age of Grace

Now, I think most serious Bible students would agree that today we are at the end of this Age of Grace. In Christendom there exists a similar condition of doubt and unbelief as was true of the people of Israel in Christ's day. Though there is a lot of expectancy among evangelical Christians, yet there is apathy, worldliness and outright attack on the Rapture subject by many others in Christendom. Doctrinal confusion is rampant, to say the least. Sectarianism permeates throughout all professing Christendom. The absolutely disgusting testimony of the Roman Catholic priesthood is heard over the newscasts almost every week—and this church is proclaimed as the largest sect of Christendom. (Of course, it is the absolute opposite of true biblical Christianity.) Protestantism has long lost its godly "protest," and liberals in Christendom even attack "the apple of God's eye," Israel, at this very crucial moment. And the real "Body of Christ"—where is it? It has become virtually indistinguishable, as its members are ignorantly mixed in with religious, Babylonian confusion. This most often robs the true Church of a great and sober opportunity for witness. It has become increasingly obvious that the vast majority of mere professors in "Christendom" are totally indifferent to the present vital issues and will be "left behind" at the Rapture of the true Church. Yes, on the skyline of most cities and towns there will still be seen the church spires, but the real Church will be gone.

The antitypical Pentecost (the resurrection and Rapture of the Church) will bring to a conclusion this Church Dispensation. Obviously, when that takes place, it will mark the *end of this Age*. However, God has actually not left us "in the dark" (1 Thess. 5:4–6) as to when this Age will close. Intelligent and spiritual Christians can easily see the stage being set for the termination of this Age and the beginning of the next. The rebirth of the nation of Israel is one obvious marker. It is also scripturally indicated by the inspired apostle Paul, in Romans chapter 11, that this Age or Dispensation of Gentile favor will end *just like the Law Age ended* as far as apostasy is concerned. Other Bible teachers have noted that both Dispensations, that of the Law and that of Grace, follow a similar pattern at the *beginning* and *conclusion* of their time periods. (We will look at this shortly.)

With this revelation from Paul in mind, we can look at the close of the Law Age and see that the culmination of Israel's *"apostasy"* involved a *"crucifixion* or *holocaust,"* a *"resurrection"* and a *"counting of days"* until *"Pentecost."* Therefore, the antitypical Pentecost—which will mark the Rapture of the Church—will also take place after the culmination of Christendom's *"apostasy"* involving a *"crucifixion* or *holocaust,"* a *"resurrection"* and a *"countdown"* until *"the Rapture."* There is no question by most conservative, Bible believing teachers that there are many indicators in world events which point to the fact that we have approached the end of this Age.

The Holocaust of Christ and the Holocaust of the Jews bear a striking resemblance. In fact, the Holocaust of the Jews of recent history has been labeled—*"The Crucifixion of The Jews"* by Jewish, Catholic and Protestant writers (see the Appendix to my study, *The*

Gospel of the Holocaust, www.SeparationTruth.com). In addition, both Holocausts are followed by a *"resurrection"* event. In our present generation there has been what has been called "the *resurrection* of the nation of Israel" after nearly two thousand years. After the resurrection of Christ, there was the "counting of days" until Pentecost and the birth of the Church. After the resurrection of the State of Israel, there has been intense interest and increasing expectancy among Christians throughout the world.

I say again, God has not left us without the necessary information and example. What happened to Jesus the Messiah has been duplicated on a social or national scale right in front of our eyes in these last days. After the "crucifixion of the Jews" and rebirth of the nation of Israel "out of the ashes of the Holocaust," as they say, we have been moving through a more significant "countdown," in the sense of intense expectancy, which leads right up to the approaching fulfillment of Pentecost.

Chapter Eleven

DISPENSATIONS and PENTECOST

Dispensational Comparisons and Contrasts

Today dispensational Bible teaching has come under attack, just as some false teachers are also ridiculing the pretribulational Rapture of the Church of Jesus Christ. I had one young man write a long list of totally confusing reasons as to why he did not believe in the Rapture of the Church occurring before the prophesied "Seventieth Week of Daniel." His arguments were filled with a conglomeration of confusing facts, all "jammed together," so that no one should even waste his time to try and sort them all out. I responded to him by saying, "If you came to my house and opened my refrigerator and pantry, and pulled out every single food item, then dumped it all into one big pile on my kitchen table, scrambled it all together, and then told me to eat it, I don't think you would find many people who would want to make the attempt! Common sense tells you certain things go together and certain things absolutely do not go together! The same thing is positively true when one uses the Scriptures—they must be 'handled properly' [2 Tim. 2:15, or as stated in the King James, 'rightly divided']." Needless to say, this young man would not qualify as a chef in anyone's restaurant. I told him that he certainly does not understand the very basics of properly handling the Scriptures.

No one should be afraid of the word "dispensation"! It is a good old English word used in the King James Version of the Bible and a few other translations. It basically carries the meaning of a "household stewardship" where one has the task entrusted to him of "dispensing" or "handing out," in an appropriate time and manner, those things assigned to the household. The steward is, in effect, the "manager" of the material things of that household. The Greek word *oikonomia*, is a compound word—*oiko* (house), and *nomia* (law or management). When the Bible is talking about a single household, *oikonomia* usually has the literal meaning of a "stewardship." Christ, Himself, gives the illustration of a stewardship in Luke 12:42—

> Who then is the *faithful* and *wise* [sensible] **steward**, whom his master will *make ruler* [put in charge] over his household, to *give them their portion* of food [rations] *in due season* [at the proper time]?

There are five particulars in this illustration which Christ gave. (1) A steward must be "*faithful*" to his master in this service. (2) A steward must be "*wise or sensible*" in his operating procedure. (3) The steward is the "ruler [*put in charge*]" of this service. (4) The steward distributes "*their portions*" to each one, (5) at the proper "*time or season*." Hence, a steward has a very responsible job as a "dispenser" of things entrusted to him "in their due season or time."

The simplest and clearest application of this word and teaching, as it would apply to this particular study, can be illustrated from Hebrews 3:1–6 and the following references. Herein, the inspired writer likens God's people to two different "households" under two different "servants" or managers. First, it says, "Moses also was faithful in all *his house*" (verse 2). This has reference to "the house of Israel." Second, it says, ". . . but Christ as a Son over *His own house*, Whose house are we . . . ." (verse 6). This, of course, has reference to the saints of the present age. In the context of Hebrews 3 there is a contrast being made. Now other Scriptures illustrate the difference between these two administrations. John 1:17 says, "For the *Law* was given through Moses, but *grace and truth* came through Jesus Christ." Then Romans 6:14 says, ". . . for you [members of the Church] are not *under Law* but *under grace*."

Hence, in Ephesians 3:2 we read—"If indeed you have heard of the *Dispensation [oikonomia] of the Grace of God*."

So it is, that when this word is used in describing a management over a city, nation or large group of people, then the words "economy," "dispensation" or "administration" are appropriate translations. By the second century of the Christian era, the Latin word, *dispensatio*, meaning "to weigh out or dispense" was used when the Greek New Testament was translated into Latin. It was also used in the popular standardized Vulgate. Several of the so-called "early church fathers" spoke of the "dispensations." I say again, when applied to the particular "household" of God's own people for a particular time period, then the word "dispensation" or "economy" is actually an accurate translation. Everyone, even the Jewish people themselves, has observed different time periods in the Bible wherein there are distinguishing elements and even ages of special "economy" which God has entrusted to men on earth. Anyone would be very foolish to ignore or deny this reality. Dispensational Bible teaching is careful to observe these different "economies."

The Bible reveals a number of different "Ages" or "Dispensations," yet only two—"The Dispensation of Law" and "The Dispensation of Grace"—actually concern the vast majority of the revelations in the Scriptures. The Hebrew Scriptures primarily focus on the Age of Law, whereas the Greek Scriptures mainly concentrate upon the Age of Grace. An interesting phenomenon in the Greek Scriptures is the fact that two of the inspired writers, John (to a lesser degree) and Paul (to a greater degree), often draw our attention to different facets of comparison between these two Dispensations. These comparisons will show certain similarities between the two Ages, but also quite often they will show striking contrasts as well.

As the signature in the beginning of a sheet of music tells us in which key it is written, so John 1:17 gives us, at the outset of the whole book, the very key in which his Gospel is written—"For *the Law* was given through Moses, but *grace and truth* came through Jesus Christ." Thus, in John, the Law and Grace are held up in contrast to one another. Though Christ was living under the Law Dispensation, yet something far different was shortly coming which is presented to the reader as being far more desirable. Christ, as to

His person, will be the fruition of all that the Law and the Prophets anticipated. John emphasized "grace and truth" principles in the ministry of Christ in contrast to the Law principles. No doubt, the Gospel of John enabled the first generation of Christians, whether Jew or Gentile, to better appreciate and recognize the distinctive revelations given by the Holy Spirit through the apostle Paul. Paul revealed a clear change from Law management to Grace management (Rom. 6:14).

In John, it is the New Birth of the Spirit which is emphasized and not the birth from the ancestral line of Abraham, Isaac and Jacob (John 3).

In John, it is the "worship" of God "in spirit and in truth" which is soon coming rather than a worship at "Jerusalem" or in the physical "Temple" (John 4).

In John, it is repeatedly the spiritual realities which are emphasized and not a physical religious program to be carried on in the future. It is the "true bread from heaven" and not the "manna" from Moses in the wilderness. It is the true "light" of the world; it is the "living water"; it is "the good shepherd," etc., etc.

And finally, it is noteworthy that in John's gospel nothing is given about being seated with Christ on the Mount of Olives, overlooking the city of Jerusalem, when He spoke of the terrible calamities coming during the future Great Tribulation, after which Messiah will come to deliver and restore Israel. Instead, in John we are seated with Christ in the quiet seclusion of the upper room at the last supper, where Christ spoke to them of His going into heaven to prepare places for them, returning to gather them to Himself and then returning with them to the "prepared places" in His Father's house (John 14:1–4).

From the letters of Paul— The History of Each Age

Many have pointed out a similarity between Moses and Paul. As Moses stood in relationship to the Law, as its steward, so Paul stands in relationship to the Dispensation of the Grace of God. Moses went up on top of Mount Sinai to receive the Law for the nation of Israel and received direct revelations from God. The apostle Paul was caught up into the "third heaven" (2 Cor. 12:1–6) to receive divine revelation from the Lord Jesus Christ concerning vital and distinctive truths for this present Age. Paul made many comparisons between the Age of Law and the Age of Grace — too many, in fact, to take up here. I will just briefly identify the major ones.

In 1 Corinthians 10:1–11, Paul was inspired to draw many "examples" between Israel under the Law with the Church under Grace today.

In 2 Corinthians 3:3–11, Paul again drew our attention to additional contrasts between some ten factors which occurred at the giving of the Law with what has taken place under the present administration of the Spirit.

In Romans 5:20 and 21, Paul stressed basic theological contrasts between the two Dispensations. (1) Under the Law the "offence abounded"; whereas, under Grace, "grace abounds"; (2) under Law, "sin reigns unto death"; whereas, under Grace, "grace reigns through righteousness"; (3) under Law, man served "in oldness of the letter"; whereas, under Grace, we "serve in newness of the Spirit."

We can thus see that the inspired apostle was moved to sometimes emphasize certain dispensational comparisons in order for us to have a clearer understanding of the actual functioning of our own Age, both in practical and doctrinal matters. One important truth which comes from this revelation is that both Ages appear to open in a similar manner. For instance, in the 1 Corinthian passage there are some obvious parallels in the beginning of both Ages. Others have pointed out this fact in the following manner:

(1) Israel was said to be "the church in the wilderness" (Acts 7:38) which had been "called-out" of Egypt. Paul speaks of it as having been "baptized unto Moses in the cloud and in the sea." The body of Christ today, on the other hand, is that company "called out" of this world system, having been supernaturally "baptized into Christ" (Gal. 3:27).

(2) Moses went up to the mountaintop to receive the revelation of the Law, whereas Paul was caught up to the third heaven to receive the revelation concerning this present economy and Age.

(3) 3000 were killed in judgment at the foot of Mount Sinai, whereas 3000 were given everlasting life on the Day of Pentecost.
(4) Israel experienced a 40 year transition period in the wilderness before entering her rest in the Land of Promise. Likewise, the Church of Jesus Christ experienced a 40 year transition period (from 30 C.E. to 70 C.E.) and reached its "maturity."
(5) During both periods of transition, they received progressive divine revelation recorded in special Scriptures written for instructions, guidance and operation.
(6) During both periods of transition, both groups received miraculous provisions to sustain them. Israel received miraculous provisions in various forms, especially for their physical sustainment. The Church of Jesus Christ received miraculous gifts of the Spirit for guidance, protection and assistance during its transition.
(7) In both cases the miraculous provisions were said to "cease." Israel's provisions ceased after they crossed over the Jordan River, whereas the Church's miraculous gifts ceased after it reached "maturity" (1 Cor. 13:10, 11 and Eph. 4:13, 14).

Some Bible teachers also point out that both Israel and the Church followed a remarkably similar course or pathway as to how their total history unfolded:

(1) Both started as a small, insignificant people.
(2) Both experienced a rise to greatness and influence.
(3) Both experienced a departure from the directions God had given to them.
(4) Both experienced a "Babylonian Captivity," for so church historians describe Christendom's defection into "Babylon's" religion.
(5) Both experienced a revival: Israel, under the leadership of Ezra and Nehemiah, and the Church, under the Protestant Reformation.
(6) Both then experienced a drifting into legalism and liberalism: Israel, under the Pharisees and Sadducees; the Church, under liberals and conservatives.

(7) Both finally succumbed to near total apostasy.

Romans 11:15–27

In this chapter the apostle Paul focused on the closing days of both the Law Age and the Age of Grace. As we observed parallels at the opening of both Ages, so we will see parallels at the closing of both Ages. The Spirit of God has laid these truths before our eyes that we may not be deceived by religious trends in apostate Christendom in these last days. Paul's revelation enables the spiritual Christian to know exactly what is going to happen at the close of this Age. Therefore believers should not be deceived into thinking some great "revival" will come at the end; this will definitely not happen! Instead, according to Paul, there will be the culmination of the prophesied great apostasy.

In this passage Paul clearly gave the revelation that both Ages or Dispensations close in a similar manner by following a similar pathway. Paul gave these truths in the context of warning Gentile people against being guilty of following the same footsteps as did the Jewish nation in its final days.

Paul then revealed that the Gentiles will indeed follow the very same path at the end of this Age of Grace as the Jews did at the close of the Law Dispensation. When that happens, not only will the Age of Grace end, but Israel will be accepted once again before God. Whereas the Gentiles are now in the forefront of God's dispensational dealings, then they will be "broken off," and Israel will once again be in the forefront of God's dispensational plan. This is a highly important revelation as to the close of our particular Dispensation and the final restoration of the nation of Israel. Paul emphasized that we should not be "ignorant" of this "mystery" (Rom. 11:25).

Paul made this revelation by an analogy. He used an olive tree with its natural branches representing Israel and wild branches representing the Gentiles, replacing the natural branches. Most interpreters agree that the base of the tree would find its representation in Abraham and the Abrahamic Covenant wherein both Jews and Gentiles find promises of acceptance before God. Though Paul started and closed this scenario with references to the Jewish people, yet the middle illustration and warning was directed toward the Gentile people. This is not an analogy concerning personal soul salvation, but rather concerning the standing of Jews and Gentiles in the outworking of God's dispensational plans. I will merely itemize the successive statements in the analogy. The top and bottom dotted lines indicate the beginning and end of the present Age.

> (1) Because of "unbelief" the natural branches (the Jewish people) are "broken off" from the place of nearness to God (vs. 17, 20).
>
> ------------------------------[30 C.E.]------------------------------
> (2) "Wild branches" (Gentiles) were "grafted in," "by faith" (vs. 17, 20).
> (3) Gentiles were not to "boast" against the discarded branches (v. 18).
> (4) Gentiles are not to be "haughty," but to "fear" (vs. 19, 20).
> (5) God "may not spare you [Gentiles] either" (vs. 21, 24).
> (6) "The fullness of the Gentiles shall come in" (v. 25).
> (7) "You [Gentiles] also will be broken off" (v. 22).
> ---------------------------[2014 + C.E.]---------------------------
>
> (8) "And they (natural branches, Jews) will be "grafted in again" (vs. 23, 24).

In order to get the fullest appreciation of this revelation, I would like to repeat the course of each Age separately under very similar statements. Each will have the slight modification of including seven statements within each Age. I will first rephrase this scenario entirely for the Jewish people under the Dispensation of the Law, then I will do the same for the Gentiles under the Age of Grace. Again the top and bottom lines of this arrangement will indicate the beginning and the end of each time period. By doing this, we will again see the similarity between the two Ages.

THE DISPENSATION OF LAW

------------------------[Approx. 1500 B.C.E.]------------------------
(1) The Jewish nation was given a favored position before God.
(2) However, they often were characterized by unbelief.
(3) They were sometimes boastful of their covenant relationship.
(4) They became prideful over Gentiles by their Abrahamic heritage.
(5) They apostatized and did not heed the warnings of the prophets.
(6) The fullness of God's dealing with then finally came.
(7) They were broken off from their place of nearness to God.
------------------------------[30 C.E.]------------------------------

(8) The Gentiles were then "grafted into" that place of nearness.

These eight statements trace the history of the Jewish nation in a similar manner as Paul does here in Romans 11. Now let us phrase this scenario entirely from the perspective of what has happened in this present Age of Gentile prominence in the favor of God.

THE DISPENSATION OF GRACE

------------------------------[30 C.E.] ------------------------------
(1) Gentile people were grafted into a place of nearness to God after Israel has been set aside.
(2) The Gentile world of professing Christendom will also come to be characterized by periods of unbelief.
(3) Professing Christendom will actually become boastful of their favored position before God.
(4) In addition, Christendom becomes prideful against the Jews and arrogant against Israel whom they supplanted.
(5) Christendom failed to take heed to the warnings of the apostles about the defection of apostasy.
(6) The "fullness of the Gentiles" will come in by the completing of the outcalling of the (saved) Gentiles for this Age.

(7) Simultaneously, the (unsaved) Gentile nations as to their dispensational standing before God are broken off.

-----------------------------[[2014 + C.E.] -----------------------------

(8) Then the natural branches, the Jewish people, will once again be grafted back into a place of nearness to God.

The Exact Close of Each Dispensation

What has happened during the recorded time of so-called "church history" stands as a clear verification of the scenario we have observed down through number (5). We have seen that there were certain similarities at the beginnings of each Dispensation, both of the Age of Law and that of the Church Age. Likewise, there have been certain similarities with the whole history of both Ages, especially also of their closing time periods. Each Age followed a similar cycle from its beginning to its end. Finally, each Age closes in apostasy.

One might ask in further detail, *exactly* how did the Law Age finally terminate, and what is the *precise* termination period of the Age of Grace? Actually many Scriptures answer the first part of this question, in essence by saying that the final total apostasy of Israel was marked by the Jewish nation's rejection of her Messiah and then His crucifixion—see Acts 2:22–24, 36; 3:13–15; 4:10–12; 7:51–53; Romans 10:1-4; 11:7–10 and verse 28. The Jewish nation was guilty of fomenting the animosity towards Christ and utilizing the cruel Roman government to execute the crime. In this regard they committed the most heinous crime which could have been committed; the Jewish nation became guilty of deicide—the rejection and death of the God-man, Jesus Christ. In final unbelief they had their own Messiah, through Whom their Covenant blessings were assured, turned over to the Roman authorities for execution. The Romans were ruthless and cruel in expediting His death.

Furthermore, the death of Jesus Christ is portrayed in the Bible as the singular greatest catastrophe ever to occur in this world. Its singularity and uniqueness are seen in Who He was and how He, the innocent Son of God, was treated. Not only did the Jewish nation and the Roman government carry out the crime but, as the Gospel of John states, "the world" was indifferent to Him (John 1:10). However, in God's overruling providence, He (Christ) became the basis for the redemption of all mankind by bearing the sins of the world. His sufferings passed out of the sight of man and He died as the "God-forsaken," antitypical "burnt sacrifice." In the Greek language His death was called a *"holocaust"* (Greek for *burnt offering*; see Heb. 10:5–10). Even the Greek translation of the Hebrew Scriptures portrayed a type of Christ—the sacrifice of Isaac—as a *holocaust*, in Genesis 22:2, 3, 6 and 7.

However, exactly three days later, Jesus Christ was spectacularly reborn and/or resurrected from the dead (Col. 1:18). And 50 days later the Church of Jesus Christ came into existence and a new Age began.

This is precisely how the Dispensation of Law terminated: Israel's apostasy was marked by the crucifixion (*holocaust*) of the Messiah, the resurrection of the Messiah, and the counting of days until Pentecost.

How will the Gentile Age Close?

And now we ask, exactly how and when will the termination of the Gentile Age take place? Is it not a fact that the final total apostasy of Christendom was marked by their cruel rejection and betrayal of the Jews in the Holocaust of recent history? Adolf Hitler merely capitalized upon the long tradition of anti-Semitism in Christendom, and even advertised it as his solace. Furthermore, Hitler chose one of the most so-called "Christian" nations on earth—Poland—as the place to finalize the crime. In 1942 Winston Churchill let it be known that a crime was being committed in the east "for which we have no name." After the war, as the world was exposed to the horror and magnitude of the crime, and in light of the burning fires in the ditches, ravines and especially at Auschwitz, it came to be called *"The Holocaust"* (burnt sacrifice). In fact, Auschwitz was also called *"Golgotha,"* and various historians—Jewish, Catholic, Protestant and even agnostic—spoke of it as *"the crucifixion of the Jews"* (see the appendix of my study, *The Gospel of the Holocaust*).

Concerning the Holocaust, the following expression has been made by Edward H. Flannery in his book, *The Anguish of the Jews*, Revised, 1985, page 295—"It is a tragedy in which Jesus participates, crucified again in the person of His people, at the hand of many baptized in His name. The sin of anti-Semitism contains many sins, but in the end it is a denial of the Christian faith, a failure of the Christian hope, and a malady of Christian love. And was not this Christianity's Supreme Defection . . . and ultimate scandal."

The Holocaust stands uniquely in all of history as a manifestation of final unbelief. The Gentile world of Christendom joined the Nazi state in what many historians recognize as the most heinous crime ever to be catalogued in the annals of human history. The rest of the world turned its back in indifference as this crime was being performed. The Gentile world actually turned its back upon the very people through whom they, themselves, were promised the ultimate blessings of God. It has now been admitted that "Christendom also committed deicide," for to reject, envy, hate and murder the Jew was the same as rejecting, hating and murdering "The Jew, Jesus Christ." As we saw in Romans 11, the apostle Paul indicated that the Gentile people would develop a hostile attitude towards the Jewish people. That is precisely what has happened to the ultimate degree.

However, exactly three years later, the nation of Israel was spectacularly reborn and/or resurrected from the dead. Many have stated in the past, and still do to this day, that "Israel was resurrected out of the ashes of the Holocaust." What happened to Jesus Christ as a singular person in terms of days, repeated itself concerning the Jewish people in terms of years. This event of the Holocaust stands absolutely, incomparably alone in all the history of civilization.

At the time of the rebirth of the nation of Israel, many evangelical Bible teachers used the expression, "the countdown has begun." By that they simply meant that the days of this present Dispensation are now numbered! This Dispensation's final act is about to close. It has also been stated that one can note that "behind the curtain, the stage is being set for the next drama—the Great Tribulation."

It is certainly true that every generation of true Christians has been living in anticipation and in expectation of the Lord's return for them. This also means that most of the things prophesied about these terminal days in preparation for Christ's return could have happened in any generation. However, it is also true that we have actually lived to see many of the world's preparations for the future end time taking place right before our eyes. Those of us who are living at the end of this Dispensation of time have an advantage of looking back over the whole panorama of "church history." From this perspective, the view is breathtaking and even shocking in its details. It is also true that we have lived to see many prophesies concerning the course of this Age take place, and now we are even seeing the stage being set for the next drama.

What remains for Christ's real Church is simply that antitypical 50th day, the Rapture! This event will close the present age wherein God has been "calling out a people from among the Gentiles for His name" (Acts 15:14).

Chapter Twelve

PERFECTION OF PENTECOST

The "Counting of Days," or "Countdown"

Most conservative, evangelical, prophetic teachers agree that the foremost event in these last days—which signals the near return of the Lord—has been the regathering of the Jewish people to their ancient homeland after being scattered throughout the world for nearly 2000 years, resulting in the creation of the State of Israel. This has been a phenomenal event on the whole world scene. In addition, Israel has been the very focal point of world attention ever since. No Christian should doubt the significance of this event. Even certain secular authorities have looked upon this as the "resurrection of the State of Israel."

Amazing as it may seem, this whole phenomenon actually began unfolding at the beginning of World War II with what has come to be called "the Holocaust of the Jews." It has been stated on numerous occasions by different people that the "resurrection of the state of Israel" has taken place "out of the ashes of the Holocaust." In this regard the concluding days of this Church's Dispensation are absolutely sobering—if not almost unbelievable—as to the reality of what has happened! Looking back at the conclusion of the Law Dispensation, we understand that "in the fullness of time" (Gal. 4:4) when Christ came into the world, Israel was in the final stages of her apostasy. What happened back then to Jesus Christ at the event of

His sufferings in terms of "days," has now happened to the Jews at this event of their suffering as a people in terms of "years."

Christ's suffering began on the tenth day of Nisan when He was selected as the antitypical Passover lamb for death. On that day of "triumphal entry" into Jerusalem, Christ cried out *"now is My soul troubled"* (John 12:27), because He knew that in reality He had actually been selected for death. Christ's physical suffering culminated *four days* later at the exact time of the Passover sacrifice. Furthermore, according to the Word of God, Christ died as a ***"holocaust"*** (whole burnt offering, Greek *holos* [whole] and *kaustos* [to burn], Heb. 10:6–10) for the sins of the world. *Three days* later He was gloriously resurrected from the dead. Then there followed the *"counting of days"* (50) until Pentecost when the Church Age was inaugurated. These were the closing days of the Law Dispensation.

Now, the close of this present Church Dispensation of time is following in the same pattern. The prophesied apostasy of Christendom certainly reached its focal point with what has come to be called "the crucifixion of the Jews," their ***"Holocaust."*** Historians say that the Holocaust, as to the actual killing of the Jews, officially began behind the cover of Germany's invasion of Russia (called Operation Barbarossa) in June of 1941. This "final solution to the Jewish question" lasted for *four years* and ended in May of 1945. However, exactly *three years* later the nation of Israel was reborn on May 14th, 1948. As I just stated, this has been called by many "the *resurrection* of the nation of Israel."

In plain language, this means that at the resurrection of the State of Israel, the "countdown" in observing the signs of these last days began. The many premillennial Bible teachers who made this observation in and after 1948, I believe, for the most part, fully realized the exactness of what they were saying. I personally remember hearing this expression—"the countdown has begun"—with my own ears, as did many others! Even the news media have reminded us of this (see as an example *The U.S. News and World Report*, Dec. 19th, 1994 and Dec. 15th, 1997). And it is true! This "countdown" has been going on for many years because alert Bible believers can see the stage being set for the next drama on the world scene—the final Great Tribulation.

First must come the Rapture! The antitypical Pentecost which will bring the Church into the presence of our blessed, long anticipated Savior will also be at the conclusion of a "countdown" of fifty—in this case, not the literal 50, *but the antitypical 50*—meaning the time of the "fullness or completion" of the "calling out of the Gentiles, a people for His name" (Rom. 11:25 and Acts 15:14). This completion must only correspond with the time that God in heaven deems "the fullness of the Gentiles" has come.

Two Human Blunders

I have personally made two mistakes in my life regarding the Rapture subject. The first, and by far the most dangerous, was early in my Christian life. At that time, as a young Christian, though I had been taught the basic pretribulational doctrine, I quickly swallowed the false teaching that the Church would go through the Great Tribulation and be raptured at the second coming of Jesus Christ. A very subtle teacher slipped into my mind a misuse of passages on the subject and, in my lack of maturity, I swallowed this error. I can also say that the confusion among the pretribulationalists, themselves, on certain passages helped encourage me in my error. Of course, I always had questions in my mind, and though I wrote many notes on the subject, there were things that I knew simply did not fit into the posttribulational scheme of things. Thankfully, God used certain patient Christian brethren to help me at that time and I have long been forgiven for this error. I thank God for their patience. That took place back in the 1950s.

The second mistake I really have no excuse for. I swallowed the suggestion, made by one of my Christian brethren, that the "50 days" between Christ's resurrection and the Feast of Pentecost were emblematic of exactly "50 years" from Israel's establishment as a nation in 1948 to her 50th anniversary in 1998. Thus the Rapture would occur on Pentecost of 1998. Of course, I should have known that the parallel of Christ's Holocaust and His resurrection with the Holocaust and the resurrection of the State of Israel should never be extended by *exactly 50 years* to the time that the Rapture of the Church would take place. In fact, I had originally made a note, which

I totally overlooked, prohibiting this. Probably I missed seeing this because of my pride. At first I thought that this time of the Rapture was only a possibility, but a year before that date I became convinced that it must be so. However, it obviously did not happen in 1998. I have since acknowledged publicly my sin and error on this matter and, again, God has forgiven me.

As to a literal 50 years passing since Israel's restoration as a nation, the 50th year came with the 50th anniversary of the nation of Israel. The first Feast day to be observed just two weeks after the 50th anniversary date of the rebirth of the nation of Israel was Pentecost on Sunday, May 31st, 1998. However, the literal 50th year was obviously not the time when the Church heard "the sound of the trumpet." And why not? *Because, as I stated at the beginning of this Bible study*, **"the Feast of Pentecost does not coincide with any historical event in the history of the nation of Israel,** as did the Feast of Passover and the Feast of Tabernacles." Therefore, the antitypical Pentecostal Rapture of the Church should never be thought to happen 50 years from the date of Israel's restoration, and certainly not to coincide with *Israel's 50th anniversary*. At that time certain other people also mistakenly thought the Rapture would occur then. As I said, originally I did not profess to know this for sure, but thought that we must just "wait and see." Nevertheless, as the time neared to that 50th anniversary of Israel, I became more convinced of it. I am thankful I did not have much time to propagate that error.

Furthermore, when we realize that the number "50" actually symbolizes "fullness" or "completion," we should never make it merely symbolize a literal **"50 years"** in time. As it relates to this Church Age, it simply symbolizes the *fullness* or *completion* of God "calling out from among the Gentiles a people for His name" (Acts 15:14), and "For I do not desire, brethren, that you should be ignorant of this mystery, lest you be wise in your own opinion, that blindness in part has happened to Israel until *the fullness* of the Gentiles has come in" (Rom. 11:25). This is precisely what it symbolizes, never the literal exact number of 50.

There are three facts I have noted regarding the Feast of Pentecost, that I had erroneously ignored at one time in the past, which should now be accentuated in order to prevent anyone from falling into the trap of "date-setting" in regard to the time of the Rapture of the Church. *First*, as noted even by Jewish sages, the Feast of Pentecost in its biblical setting was not connected to any historical event in Israel's early history. Therefore, they even regarded it as sort of a "mystery" festival only identified by the counting of days and weeks. *Second*, as given in the Hebrew Scriptures, there was actually no month and calendar date set for Pentecost. *Third*, the counting of days and weeks to the number of 50 has reference simply to the "fullness of time" for whatever purpose God has in view. Therefore, one should never relate the prophetic fulfillment of Pentecost to any time or event in Israel's history, and certainly not to the literal number of 50 used in the observance of Pentecost. These important facts and reality make Pentecostal typology immune from "date-setting" and allow it to still be compatible with the doctrine of *imminency* in the expectancy of the Rapture coming of Christ.

However, I did not stop preaching the truth about the pretribulational Rapture of the Church simply because I was personally mistaken about it many years ago. In fact, becoming clear about my own error helped me to be clearer in teaching the subject. In a similar manner, I do not believe that my second mistake should cloud the beauty of God's truth on the subject of *"The Pentecostal Rapture of The Church."* That truth will stand regardless of my careless failure. I have since studied carefully every detail of the biblical truths encompassed within this area of revelation. Once I saw the *"leaven"* and extricated it, I therefore finally decided to share the truth of this subject in its purity. It is too beautiful and clear to pass over because of a human error. In fact, I believe the truth will be emphasized brighter than ever before.

The "Divine, Perfect Consummation of Time"

How many times has Romans 8:18–39 been read at the bedsides of saints who were struggling in the closing days and hours of their earthly sojourns? A great many times, I am sure! I have personally done so several times as I attempted to bring consolation to the spirits of those who would soon depart this life. There is hardly any chapter in the Bible which conveys the assurances of God to the hearts of His children as does this passage of Scripture. The comfort that these truths offer focuses upon the blessed promises of God for the ultimate Jubilee of liberation from the bondage of our mortal bodies to our receiving glorified bodies at that great resurrection time. Paul's words stir our souls in anticipation.

> *For I consider that the sufferings of this present time are not worthy to be compared with the glory which shall be revealed in us.* (Rom. 8:18)

Paul says the liberation and resurrection of the saints will be so glorious that even the physical creation itself anticipates the curse being lifted from its own struggle in bondage and futility.

> *For the earnest expectation of the creation eagerly waits for the revealing of the sons of God.... because the creation itself also will be delivered from the bondage of corruption into the glorious LIBERTY of the children of of God.* (vs.19–21)

In giving these promises, the apostle Paul is utilizing the blessed 50th year Jubilee *release* as it was written in the Law of Moses. Like the Feast days themselves being prophetic, so the Jubilee year as well looks forward to that blessed end time of "proclamation of liberty throughout all the land" (Lev. 25:10, Rom. 8:21). (See also *The Book of Leviticus,* by Kellogg, pages 512-514 and *Unger's Bible Handbook,* page 120.) The Jubilee not only spoke of liberty for those who were sold into bondage, but also the restoration of the land. Thus, Paul's portrayal of the coming "glorious liberty of the children of God" from the "bondage of corruption" also anticipated the eventual restoration of the whole earth which is now groaning in agony. Such glimpses of future glory are revitalizing to our souls — "for we walk by faith and not by sight" (2 Cor. 5:7).

Paul amplifies this truth by the second typology of the same prophetic principle. We should remember that the calculation for the Jubilee year and for the Feast of Pentecost Day is on the same basis — seven weeks plus one = 50. (See also the *Davis Dictionary of The Bible,* under Jubilee.) When we continue to read from Paul in Romans 8:22 and 23 we will see that both these typologies are now spoken of in the same context—

> *For we know that the whole creation groans and labors with birth pangs together until now. And not only that, but we also who have the* **Firstfruits of the Spirit***, even we ourselves groan within ourselves, eagerly waiting for the adoption, the redemption of our body.*

So the physical creation will eventually experience its typical 50th year release from the bondage of the curse. However, in this context, the 50th year Jubilee for the earth will not happen until after God first grants the antitypical 50th year resurrection of His saints from the bondage of corruption, i.e., the Rapture of the Church.

By these words Paul confirms the Rapture truth by both the 50th year "Jubilee" and the 50th day of the "Feast of Firstfruits." The believers who possess the "Firstfruits of the Spirit" guarantee are, in effect, counting off the 50 days until the "Harvest," in anticipation of the glorious resurrection of our bodies. Thus, God's promise of our glorification, whether typified in 50 years or 50 days, will be wonderfully accomplished.

> *For we were saved in this hope, but hope that is seen is not hope; for why does one still hope for what he sees? But if we hope for what we do not see, then we eagerly wait for it with perseverance.* (Rom. 8:24 and 25)

Therefore, there should be no question in our minds that the resurrection and Rapture of the Church of Jesus Christ are beautifully prefigured by the typology of Pentecost, and even of the 50 day counting until Pentecost, when the two loaves were waved up in the air. Most certainly, whether in the principle of the 50th day, or in the particulars of the ritual offering, the Rapture is prefigured by Pentecost. The question that stirs our souls is not, "Will there be?" but, "*When* will be the Pentecostal Rapture of the Church of Jesus Christ?" In the context of Romans 8, the Spirit of God does not appear to be informing us that the antitypical Pentecost will fall upon a *literal* Jubilee year in Israel. It was true that the particular Pentecost which fell upon a Jubilee year in Israel was in 1998. As I have acknowledged, the Holy Spirit certainly did not set that date for the Rapture of the Church. The Holy Spirit has *set a date all right!* But that date is the perfect timing which God alone knows, when the "fullness (50th) of the Gentiles has come in." In turn, the Rapture of the Church will take place on schedule.

The reason this is true should be obvious to all! This particular Firstfruits Harvest Feast has literally been named by the exact *time period* of its observance—"Weeks" or "Pentecost (50th)." After the counting of seven weeks, on the fiftieth day they were to offer two loaves of bread as a "New Grain Offering" to be "waved" in the air before the Lord. The spiritual significance of the date of its observance is a main feature in its observance and in the typology!

The Holy Spirit has further signified through the apostle Paul that the close of the Dispensation of the Grace of God is parallel with and similar to the close of the Dispensation of Law. The factual observation of a very clear parallel, which has been taking place in these closing years, points to an antitypical "Pentecost" on our doorstep. The close of both Ages involves an "apostasy," a "crucifixion or holocaust," a "resurrection," a "countdown" and finally, a "Pentecost." Therefore, the one primary purpose of this study is to examine the revelation about "Pentecost" and the potential of the soon coming *Pentecostal Rapture of the Church of Jesus Christ*!

"The Dispensation of The Fullness of Times"

In Ephesians 1:7–10 the apostle Paul used the expression which designates an economy of time of God's dealing with mankind. The expression is—*"The Dispensation of the Fullness of Times."* The determination of exactly which dispensation the apostle Paul has in view has been discussed by different Bible teachers, usually in a friendly manner. It either has reference to the present *Dispensation of Grace* or to the future *Dispensation of the Kingdom* when Christ reigns on earth for one thousand years. I have most often seen it interpreted by dispensational teachers as referring to the future Messianic Kingdom. Yet some teachers are not at all confident of this. One older Bible teacher, whom I personally knew and have deep respect for, one time—in the midst of a discussion among us—looked at the passage with a questioning eye and then, thinking out loud, said, "in all probability, it does have reference to the *present Age of Grace*." I have since seen several traditional commentaries which, without any doctrinal prejudice, take it as a clear reference to, as they would say, "the present Gospel Age."

The context of the passage indicates that in this period of time it is God's purpose to "head up all things in Christ." Allow me to quote the passage here by a literal rendering:

> In Whom we have redemption through His blood, the forgiveness of trespasses, according to the riches of His grace, which He made to abound toward us in all wisdom and intelligence, making known to us the mystery of His will, according to His good pleasure which He purposed in Himself, *for the Stewardship* [Dispensation] *of the Fullness of Times,* to **head up** all things in Christ, the things in the heavens and things on the earth. (Eph. 1:7–10)

I now believe that we can determine that the present Church Age is very definitely in view by three facts: <u>one</u>, everything is stated in the present tense for our personal benefit now in this present Age; <u>two</u>, other statements in the immediate context; and <u>three</u>, by comparing it with a similar statement from Paul's epistle to the Colossians.

As to number <u>two</u>, the immediate context goes on to tell us extensively what things we have "in Him" right now which are actually in compliance with the same terminology. "*In Whom we were also chosen as His inheritance*" (Verse 11). And that God has "*put all things under His feet and gave* **Him to be <u>head</u> over all things to the Church,** *which is His body, the <u>fullness</u> of Him Who fills all things*" (Verses 22 and 23). God has obviously made Christ "*Head* *over all things . . . to the Church*" right now in this present age. In addition, Christ is right now "*the fullness of Him*" in the heavens.

As to number <u>*three*</u>, Paul uses similar terminology in Colossians 1:19 and 20, which is clearly in the present tense as a present reality—

> For it pleased the Father that in Him ***all fullness should dwell***, and by Him to reconcile all things to Himself, whether things on earth or things in heaven.

This present "*fullness*" of Christ as stated in both Ephesians and Colossians is therefore apropos to the Ephesian statement (1:10) about this Age being designated as "*the Dispensation of the Fullness of Times.*"

Consequently, we can understand that in the present age God has indeed "*headed up all things in Christ*," including the reconciliation of "*things in the heavens and things on the earth.*" In a very proper sense, therefore, the present age is in view, and is designated as "the Dispensation of the *Fullness* of Times." This fact enhances my initial thesis that the Feast of Pentecost, which means *completion or fullness,* is actually typical of the present Age—this age being designated as "*the completion or fullness of time.*"

Fullness or Completion

We saw in chapters four and five that the number 50 as used in Scripture signifies a perfect *fullness* or *completion* for whatever purpose God has in view. We also observed that the name "Pentecost" itself means "fiftieth." Therefore, literally it would mean the day of "fullness or completion" as to its spiritual significance.

Acts 2:1, which was quoted at the very beginning of this study, states "When the Day of Pentecost had *fully come, . . .*" The Greek word for "fully come" is *sumpleroo*, which is a compound word, *sum*, meaning "completely," and *pleroo,* meaning "to fill." Hence, together the word literally means **"to completely fill."** This also gives us the spiritual significance of the numeral 50 as used in the Scriptures, as simply speaking of "fullness or completion." Some other translations of this verse draw attention to this fact. Alford, for instance, in his *New Testament for English Readers*, would translate it "while the day of Pentecost was being *fulfilled*." Rotherham, in his *Emphasized Bible*, states, "while the day of Pentecost was *filling up* [the number of days]." The *New American Standard Bible* renders it, "When the day of Pentecost was *completed*."

This fact of translation demonstrates for us that the important significance of this Feast Day points directly to what happened on that day in the plan and arrangement of Almighty God—that is, the creation of the Church of our Lord Jesus Christ by the baptism of the Holy Spirit which immediately took place.

In addition, this Greek word *pleroo* or *pleroma* is used on other occasions, two of which are important to this study. As was quoted already, Ephesians 1:10 states that this present Age or Dispensation is designated as "the Dispensation of the *Fullness* [Greek, *pleroma*] *of Times*." In other words, we could call this Age "the Pentecostal Dispensation." Not only was the Church born on the Day of Pentecost, but the spiritual truth of all *fullness dwelling in Christ* actually characterizes this age.

Last, this same word is used in Romans 11:25 where Paul uses "fullness" (*pleroma*) in describing the conclusion of the "calling out" of the Gentiles as a "people for His name." Notice two passages in sequence—

> (Acts 15:14) Simon [Peter] has declared how God at the first [Acts 10] visited the *Gentiles to take out of them a people for His name*.

> (Rom. 11:25) For I do not desire, brethren, that you should be ignorant of this mystery, lest you should be wise in your own opinion, that blindness in part has happened to Israel until the *fullness* [*pleroma*] *of the Gentiles has come in*.

Since, as I have demonstrated in this study, Pentecost is actually prophetic of the future resurrection and Rapture of the Church of Jesus Christ, then it follows that when the "fullness [50th]" of the "out-calling of the Gentiles" comes in, then the antitypical Pentecost, or the prophetic aspect of Pentecost, will be "completed." This is the precise time and event when the present Dispensation will be terminated. Consequently, we can understand Paul's words in Romans 11:25 as meaning—"When the antitypical *Pentecost* [*pleroma*] takes place, this Age will close."

The beginning planting of this *new field of grain* began on Pentecost in the second chapter of the book of Acts, and the harvesting of this whole field will take place at the *Rapture of the Church* as described in 1 Thessalonians 4:13–18 and Romans 11:25. Pentecost is the Harvest Feast of Firstfruits and the Church of Jesus Christ has the "Firstfruits of the Spirit."

And immediately after this, Paul spoke of—

The Restoration of Israel

One of the most amazing things about Shavuot (Pentecost) is that its prophetic conclusion not only takes the Church into heaven, but it also brings about the restoration of the nation of Israel back into God's favored position. This has been demonstrated several ways:

(1) In the book of Ruth, we noted earlier that the conversion of this Gentile woman, and her reception during the spring harvest season actually became the basis for her to act as a "restorer of life" (Ruth 4:15) to a Jewish family. Thus the typology also speaks of the restoration of Israel.
(2) We also noted that chronologically, some 50 days after Israel's exodus out of Egyptian bondage (Exo. 19:1–11) the Law was given from Mount Sinai. Though Israel did not observe Shavuot during its wilderness journey, nevertheless, the 50 days having transpired from the Passover to the giving of the Law can be seen as symbolic of the activating of the Law system after the Rapture of the Church.
(3) After the creation of the State of Israel in 1948, we saw that its 50th anniversary occurred in 1998, and *the first Feast* to be observed two weeks later was *Pentecost*. So Pentecost was then

celebrated for the Jews with a view to the commemoration of its 50th anniversary.

(4) Here in Romans 11 the apostle Paul positively ties in the restoration of Israel immediately after the "fullness of the Gentiles has come in"—

> ... until the fullness of the Gentiles has come in [i.e., the Rapture]. ***And so all Israel shall be saved***, as it is written; 'The Deliverer will come out of Zion, and He will turn away ungodliness from Jacob; for this is my covenant with them, when I take away their sins.' ...

And then Paul concludes with that marvelous acknowledgment,

> *Oh, the depth of the riches both of the wisdom and knowledge of God! How unsearchable are His judgments and His ways past finding out!* (Rom. 11:26, 27 and 33.)

In conclusion, as I stated at the very beginning of this study, Acts 2:1 and 2 will be prophetically fulfilled at the Rapture. The antitypical Pentecost will have fully come, there will have been the shout (sound) from heaven, and we will now all be in one accord in one place—with Christ!

ADDENDUM

20 REASONS FOR *THE PRETRIBULATIONAL RAPTURE OF THE CHURCH*

By Jack W. Langford
(Who at one time sincerely believed in
the posttribulational Rapture of the Church)

First given in 1982,
Revised in 1997 and 2007
Present edition, 2014

Defining the Rapture

First of all, it would be appropriate to define what the Rapture of the Church is and explain what makes it unique. The Rapture of the Church of Jesus Christ is the sudden translation of both the resurrected dead and the living Church saints out of this world. This is to take place at the coming of the Lord for the Church at the close of this particular Age or Dispensation. There are two main passages given by the apostle Paul which explain this to us. The first is from Paul's first inspired letter to the new Christians of Thessalonica—1 Thessalonians 4:13–18. In this passage it is revealed that both the resurrected dead saints of this Age and those saints alive on earth at the time of Christ's coming for the Church will suddenly be **"caught up together . . . to meet the Lord in the air.** And thus we shall always be with the Lord." In the very next chapter Paul indicated that this glorious event will happen in proximity to "the Day of the Lord" (1 Thess. 5). The second passage is from Paul's first letter to the Corinthian church, 1 Cor. 15:51–57. Herein we are told that this catching up of the Church was a "mystery," meaning it was not known in past Ages (see also Col. 1:26, 27). It will involve a change in our bodies from "mortality to immortality" and will occur very suddenly, as in "the twinkling of an eye."

The word **"rapture"** is taken from the older, much used, Latin translation of the Bible from the Latin verb *"rapto"* of 1 Thessalonians 4:17—"to be caught up or raptured." This "catching away" of the Church is commonly called "The Rapture of the Church." The Greek word *"harpazo"* simply means "to snatch or catch away." It is used elsewhere in Scripture when the evangelist Philip was suddenly, miraculously transported from one spot in Palestine to another place many miles away (Acts 8:39). It is also used of Paul being suddenly transported into the "third heaven" (2 Cor. 12:2, 4). In the book of Revelation it is used of Christ ("the Man Child") being caught away "into heaven" (Rev. 12:5). In the case of the Rapture of the Church, it means that the total members of the Church, "the body of Christ," both dead and living, will be suddenly transported into the air to meet Christ at His coming and then, as we shall see, to be taken by Him into heaven.

There are many other references in Paul's letters which talk about this stupendous event as the abiding and ever present "hope" of the Church of Jesus Christ. This has earnestly been anticipated by every generation of true Christians. Since this is a clear prophecy of the future blessing for the Church, it has naturally been asked, "When will it happen? Will it happen after the great prophesied worldwide calamities of the last days—'The Great Tribulation'—or will it happen earlier in its own distinct time??" The purpose of this Bible study is to show that the Rapture of the Church will happen before the prophesied Great Tribulation and Day of the Lord's wrath. In other words, the simple order in which it is first revealed in 1 Thessalonians—first, the Rapture (Chap.4), and then "the Day of the Lord" (Chap.5)—is the actual order in which these two events will occur.

Dispensational Distinctions

To understand this event, one must first understand that in the Bible there are different time periods revealed called "Ages" or "Dispensations," during which there are different economies in

God's dealing with mankind. The pretribulational Rapture of the Church is the normal position or outgrowth of Dispensational Bible teaching. For further information about this, please see the chart and explanation of the Dispensations called *The Rightly Dividing Chart* which can be found on my web site *SeparationTruth.com*. All Bible students must believe in the different "Ages", "Dispensations" or "Stewardships" which the Bible speaks about; this is fundamental. True enough, many teachers try to twist these various time periods around to suit their theories. Nevertheless, we need to be familiar with them in order to understand this present Age in which we live.

The fact that one must recognize a distinct economy or "stewardship" for this particular "mystery" time period, in contrast to the past Age of the Law and the future Messianic Kingdom of 1000 years, will automatically also mean that there should be a distinct and separate conclusion to this present Age which is not revealed in the Hebrew Scriptures nor is a major theme in the Gospel accounts. The dispensational distinctions between the Ages or economies in God's dealing with mankind also mean one should consistently recognize different characteristics in the scriptural descriptions about the termination of each Age.

It is also fundamental, when one reads the Bible on this subject, to recognize the distinctive ministry of the apostle Paul for this present Church Age. The special revelations about the Church Age (Eph. 3:1–7) are given through the apostle Paul—who is also noted as "the Apostle to the Gentiles," in contrast to the other twelve apostles who were distinctly called "to the circumcision" or Israel (see Gal. 2).

With these very brief preliminary thoughts, we will begin our trek through the various proofs that the Church of Jesus Christ will be "caught up" or "raptured" out of this earth prior to the prophesied time of Great Tribulation coming upon mankind. Please check up and read all the Scriptures which will be given in order to prove for yourself, as a "noble Berean" (Acts 17:11), whether these things are so. I have changed the order of these "Reasons" from when I first gave them in 1982, so as to give a better sequential perspective.

I will try to make these 20 Reasons brief, yet clear enough for self-explanation.

REASON NO. I

The Rapture is Missing from the Resurrection Prophesies of the Hebrew Scriptures

The Hebrew Scriptures spelled out very clearly that there was to be a resurrection from the dead of all saints of past ages. Some of the Greek Scriptures added to this line of prophecy about the resurrection of the Old Testament saints. The final book of Revelation even adds that the saints who die during the Great Tribulation will be raised at the very same time as the Old Testament saints. These prophecies tell plainly exactly when this particular resurrection will occur. These prophecies say nothing whatsoever about the translation of the living saints of this Age, i.e., the Rapture of the Church.

1. Job 19:25–27 When the Redeemer <u>stands upon the earth</u> in the latter days.
2. Isaiah 25:6–9 When the Messiah <u>restores</u> all things.
3. Isaiah 26:19–21 At the conclusion of Messiah's <u>indignation</u>.
4. Hosea 13:9–14 When the great King will <u>save</u> <u>Israel</u>.
5. Daniel 12:1–3 At the time of the "<u>end</u>" of the tribulation period.
6. Daniel 12:13 At the "<u>end</u>" of the prophesied days of Israel's trouble.
7. John 11:24 At the "<u>last</u> <u>day</u>".
8. Luke 14:14 Rewards at the <u>resurrection</u> <u>of</u> <u>the just</u>.
9. Rev. 11:18 Time of <u>the dead</u> (saints) to be <u>judged and rewarded</u>.
10. <u>Rev. 20:4–6</u> After <u>Great</u> <u>Tribulation, at</u> <u>the</u> <u>beginning</u> <u>of</u> <u>the</u> <u>Millennium</u>.

Please read all these passages carefully. There is one thing common to all these passages and that is the fact that the Rapture of the Church of Jesus Christ is MISSING! It is simply not to be found! That there is the resurrection of all the Old Testament saints to glorified life **on earth** is factual. That the Tribulation saints join this resurrection from the dead is also factual. That this resurrection occurs at the very end of the Great Tribulation at the second coming of the Jewish Messiah to rule and reign on earth is factual. That these passages talk about the unique translation of Church saints, both those who are resurrected from the dead and the living saints, into the air to meet Christ and return with Him to heaven IS NOT FACTUAL—IS NOT GIVEN—IS MISSING from all these passages. No matter how one reads these passages, the Rapture is simply not to be found. The only conclusion is that the Rapture is distinct and different. Likewise, since it is MISSING—NOT THERE—**it could only have happened at an earlier date**!

REASON NO. II

The Church is not in the Prophesied 70 Weeks of Daniel

In the 9th chapter of Daniel, verses 20–27, God reveals the future time clock for the nation of Israel, from Daniel's time until the Messiah's death and second coming. These "70 weeks" of "years" equal 490 years of history for Israel. In addition, in several places the book of Daniel speaks extensively about this future final 70th week. See the chart below. The simple fact, which anyone can observe, is that the Church which is Christ's body is nowhere found in this time period. It is most certainly NOT in the first 69 weeks of years because it was not created until after the death of Christ, NOR is it found anywhere in the book of Daniel so as to be placed in this final 70th week. The Church is parenthetical in nature to these events. It is MISSING!

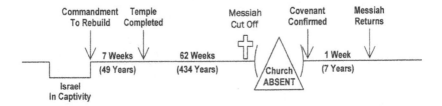

REASON NO. III

The Rapture of the Church is not found in MATTHEW 3, 13, 24 or 25

These are the great prophetic passages of Matthew which speak of the Messiah's coming to reign in the future Kingdom on earth in the last days. Each passage clearly spells out what will happen to **the saints** who are alive during that immediate time period. Once again, in all these passages you will NOT find the Rapture of the Church; it is simply not there! Once again, it is MISSING!

1. Matt. 3:10–12 John the Baptist is here predicting the coming judgment by the Messiah. The saints are represented by the "good fruit trees" which are left standing, whereas the dead trees are thrown into the fire (verse 10). The same is represented in verse 12, by the gathering of the wheat (saints) into the barns (i.e., the Kingdom). The unsaved (chaff) are destroyed as with fire. See also Malachi 4:1, 2. *There is No Rapture!*

2. Matt. 13 The parable of the wheat and tares (24–30, 36–43) teaches a similar truth. The righteous grow up during the Tribulation period ministry. The tares also grow up, but at the harvest they are first gathered and burned in the fire, whereas the righteous are gathered into the Kingdom on earth. *There is no Rapture!*

3. Matt.24 Prophecy of the Great Tribulation and second coming of Christ. Note once again that the wicked are taken in judgment whereas the righteous are left (36-41). Israel, God's elect are regathered (v.31) in fulfillment of Deut. 30:1–6. Once again, *There is no Rapture!*

4. Matt.25 This speaks of the judgment of the nations at the second coming of Messiah (31–46). The sheep

and goats are representative of two classes of people—goats, the unsaved, and sheep, the saved. The <u>sheep</u> are those who served God during the Tribulation period. Now they are rewarded <u>entrance into the Kingdom.</u> The <u>goats</u> are cast <u>out</u>. Again, *There is no Rapture!*

None of the "saints" in any of the episodes of Matthew's prophetic accounts are said to be "glorified" in any way, nor are they "caught up" in the air to meet Christ. They are all simply gathered into the Kingdom of the Messiah at the time of His return. All these accounts are complete in and of themselves. There are saved and unsaved. And then, there are the saved going into the Messianic Kingdom. Since the Church is not found in these passages, nor is the Rapture found in any of these passages, the Rapture of the Church must have taken place sometime before these events take place. Very plainly, the Rapture of the Church does not take place at the end of the Great Tribulation period at the second coming of the Messiah to reign in His Kingdom on earth.

REASON NO. IV

The Church was a "Mystery," not previously revealed

The apostle Paul specifically says that the Church of Jesus Christ was a "mystery not known in other ages"—see Ephesians 3:1–7. This "mystery" had to do with both the <u>character</u> of what the Church is, and the <u>time duration</u> or Dispensation of its existence. The Church is composed of saved Jews and saved Gentiles, baptized by the Spirit into "one body" to form **"one new man"** (see I Cor. 12:13 and Eph. 2:11–17).

Thus the Church, as an Age time period, or as a distinct company of people, was not known by the Hebrew prophets, nor was it immediately in view during the ministry of Christ on earth. It was distinctly revealed through the apostle Paul as these Scriptures state (see also Col. 1:26, 27 and Rom. 16:25). The "mystery" character of the Church demands an exclusiveness from God's revealed program for the nation of Israel as revealed in the Hebrew Scriptures, the Synoptic Gospels and the Book of Revelation. When you look at particular prophecies in the Old Testament about the first and second coming of Christ, you will not find the Church nor the Church Age. As examples—

<u>Isaiah 61:1–4</u> (Lk. 4:16–20)   Two comings, but—no Church!
<u>Isaiah 11:1–6</u>   Two comings, but—no Church!
<u>Zechariah 9:9, 10</u>   Two comings, but—no Church!
<u>Malachi 3:1–3</u>   Two comings, but—no Church!

REASON NO. V

The "Mystery" Character of the Rapture Itself

As the Church and the Church Age were "mysteries" not revealed in the past, so the very Rapture of the Church, itself, is a "mystery" as well. Its unique characteristics cannot be equated with any other event.

In 1 Corinthians 15:51–54 the apostle Paul says of the Rapture, "Behold, I show you a mystery." This means that the Rapture was a sacred secret not revealed in other ages. In 1 Thessalonians 4:13–18 the apostle Paul says of the Rapture, "This we say unto you by the Word of the Lord." Paul did not mean he was quoting the Old Testament or the Gospels. Like the prophets who had the Word of the Lord come to them, so it was with Paul and his companions. This was the Word of God coming to them about this new, unique revelation.

In Colossians Paul speaks of the totality of this revelation which culminates in our glorification. Colossians 1:26, 27, ". . . the **mystery which has been hidden from ages and from generations,** but now has been revealed to His saints. To whom God willed to make known what are the riches of the glory of this mystery among the Gentiles: which is **Christ in you, the hope of glory.**"

In Ephesians 5:26, 27 and 32 Paul speaks of the unique presentation of the Church to Christ as a part of this great mystery. Certainly the mysterious character of the Rapture of the Church gives the Church a distinctive place in its final disposition. Note the chart below—

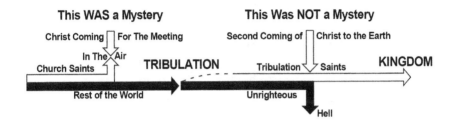

REASON NO. VI

The Unique Promises of John 14 Compared with 1 Thessalonians 4

When one reads the great prophecy chapter of Matthew 24, he will be impressed with the fact that the apostles are situated on top of the Mount of Olives looking down upon the city of Jerusalem, wondering about her future. Christ speaks of saints of that future time who will be finally rescued after passing through the calamitous times of the Great Tribulation with all its specified pestilences, wars, warnings of false prophets, signs, world events, actions of the Antichrist and finally, the earth literally being shaken from its foundations in cataclysmic judgment.

Not so, when one comes to John chapter 14. Here one finds himself in the calm seclusion of an evening meal, with Jesus warmly and beautifully explaining His return for His own. There are no signs, no earthshaking events, no Antichrist, no pestilences, earthquakes or fearful events—only the breathtaking suspense of our destination in heaven. What an amazing difference! Let us note the parallel with **1 Thessalonians 4**—

John 14:1–41	Thessalonians 4:13–18
1. "Let not your heart be troubled"	"that you sorrow not"
2. "believe in Me"	"this we say unto you by the Word of the Lord"
3. "In My father's house"	"from Heaven . . ."
4. "I will come again"	"the coming of the Lord"
5. "I will receive you unto Myself"	"caught up to meet the Lord in the air"
6. "where I am there, you may be also"	"so shall you ever be with the Lord"
7. "let not your heart be troubled"	"comfort one another with these words"

The three distinct and important aspects of this passage are: (1) Christ is going into heaven to His Father's mansion; (2) in heaven Christ is going to be preparing residences for the believers; and (3) Christ will come again to receive the believers to Himself, and take them into heaven with Him to these prepared residences.

Obviously, the truths of this revelation cannot be forced to fit into the contrasting scenario, as described in Matthew 24, when Christ returns to reign on earth.

REASON NO. VII

The Unique Presentation of the Church Into Heaven

It is evident from the Scriptures which we have already read that the Church has a unique hope in the heavens. In Colossians 1:5 this truth is repeated, "For the hope which is laid up for you in <u>heaven</u>." There are three things which are going to happen when the Church is caught up into heaven at the Rapture.

(1) The first thing that will happen is **The Bodily Perfection** of the whole Church collectively. This is her resurrection and transformation into bodies like that of Christ (Rom. 8:23; 1 Cor. 15:45–53; Philip. 3:20, 21 and 1 John 3:2).

(2) The next event is **The Bema Purging** of the whole Church. "Bema" is simply the Greek word for Judgment Seat. The Church will stand before the judgment seat of Christ (see Rom. 14:10; 1 Cor. 3:13–15; 2 Cor. 5:10). This judgment obviously requires an extended period of time. It will involve the final cleansing for the Church. This is all totally distinct from the judgment which will occur between the saved and lost on earth at the second coming of Messiah to reign over Israel and the world.

(3) Then there is **The Bridal Presentation** of the Church to Christ in the heavenlies. This is revealed in 2 Corinthians 11:2; Ephesians 5:25–27, 32; and Colossians 1:21, 22. This should not be confused with the great wedding event to take place on earth between redeemed Israel and the Messiah when He comes to reign.

These events could not take place at the very same time as those events prophesied to take place at the second coming of Christ to reign on the earth.

REASON NO. VIII

The Restrainer Removed Prior to the Day of the Lord

At the precise moment the Holy Spirit took up His residence upon the earth on the Day of Pentecost some 2000 years ago, the Church of Jesus Christ was instantly born. One moment, there was just a group of believers praying; the next moment the Church was created by the sudden unique presence of the Holy Spirit and His "baptizing them into one body" (Acts 1:5 and 1 Cor. 12:13). One moment the Church was not there; the next moment, it was there! This is how this present Age began. Conversely, we can understand with the same biblical certainty that, when the Holy Spirit removes Himself "from the midst" of this earth, the Church will be removed with Him. The Spirit and the Church are uniquely bound up together at this time. Romans 8:11 says, "But if the **Spirit** of Him Who raised up Jesus Christ from the dead **dwells in you**, He Who raised up

Christ from the dead will also **give life to your mortal bodies through His Spirit Who dwells in you.**"

When the collective body of Christ, which was "baptized by the Spirit into one body" (1 Cor. 12:13), ascends suddenly into the air to meet Jesus Christ, the Holy Spirit, Who uniquely composes that body, will be the *very instrument of power* by which all believers ascend into glory. Thus, the Holy Spirit will simultaneously ascend with them and in them. One moment the Church will be here—*the next instant it will be G-O-N-E!*

Now in 2 Thessalonians 2:1–10 we are precisely told of the removal of the Holy Spirit from the midst of the earth, and also just exactly when He will remove Himself. Thus, we have information to tell us when this Rapture will occur. In this chapter the apostle Paul tells us there is One "restraining" the appearance of the Antichrist (vs. 6, 7) until He removes Himself. The identity of this Restraining One was no mystery to the Thessalonians. Paul says, "and now you know what is restraining . . . He Who is now restraining." The identity of this Restrainer should also be no mystery to us. It is the Holy Spirit of God. How do we know that?

(1) The Holy Spirit has always been a restraining force against evil. When the world came to be in rebellion against God in Noah's day, God said, "My Spirit will not always strive with men" (Gen. 6:3). When the Holy Spirit ceased restraining evil, judgment came. In the age of Israel's nationhood, the Spirit often restrained the enemies, "When the enemy came in like a flood, the Spirit of the Lord shall lift up a standard against him" (Isa. 59:19). And the Spirit acted as a restraint against Israel, herself, "But they rebelled, and vexed His Holy Spirit" (Isa. 63:10). Likewise, concerning the present Age, Christ said, "And when He is come [the Holy Spirit], He will *reprove the world of sin*, and *of righteousness*, and *of judgment*" (John 16:8).

(2) The present ministration of the Holy Spirit is also called "the ministration of righteousness" (2 Cor. 3:7–9, R.V., lit. trans.). It clearly stands in opposition to the administration of lawlessness under Antichrist. "The mystery of lawlessness is already at work" Paul said (2 Thess. 2:7). Yet the Antichrist will eventually minister "lawlessness" as "the man of lawlessness" (2 Thess. 2:3) without restraint. Obviously, the full unleashing of "lawlessness," without

restrictions, cannot go into effect until the impediment by "the ministration of righteousness" ceases. You can have degrees of lawlessness during the "reign of righteousness" (Rom. 5:21), and you can even have some righteousness during the "reign of lawlessness." However, you cannot have "the *reign* of lawlessness" and "the *reign* of righteousness" at the same time because two conflicting ministrations cannot function simultaneously. Thus, as long as the "ministration of the Spirit" continues, the reign of Antichrist will be held back. When the Holy Spirit "removes [Himself] out of the midst," then the Antichrist will "be revealed" and reign.

(3) A parallel passage is 1 John 4:2–4. "Hereby know ye **the Spirit of God** . . . every spirit that does not confess that Jesus Christ has come in the flesh is not of God: and this is **the spirit of Antichrist,** whereby you have heard that he should come; and even now already is in the world. . . . because **greater is He** [the Holy Spirit] Who is in you, **than he** [the spirit of Antichrist] that is in the world."

This Scripture is similar to Paul's words in 2 Thessalonians 2. (a) Paul said, "the mystery of lawlessness is already at work"; John said, "the spirit of Antichrist . . . is already in the world." (b) Paul said, the lawless one will yet be "revealed in his own time"; John said, "you have heard that he should come." (c) Paul said, there is a greater One Who is now "restraining"; John said, "greater is He Who is in you than he that is in the world." Language could hardly be any plainer as to Whom the "Restrainer" is.

(4) The One restraining in verse 6 of 2 Thessalonians 2 is spoken of in the neuter gender, "*that* which is restraining." Yet, in verse 7, the same is spoken of in the masculine gender, "*He* Who now restrains. . . . *He* removes out of the way." This gender switch is actually one of the evidences to the identity of the Holy Spirit. The word "spirit" in the Greek language is in the neuter gender and, therefore, on a few occasions the neuter gender is used (see also Rom. 8:16 and 26). However, the person of the Spirit is usually spoken of by the masculine gender pronoun, "He" (John 14:26; 15:26; 16:7–15, etc.).

(5) Remember, the rebellion of Antichrist is no ordinary rebellion. Satan himself, personally on earth, will be energizing the Antichrist. Legions of fallen angels will assist. Demons will be

unleashed. Nations of earth will be supportive. This is the climactic rebellion of Lucifer. There simply is no human being, government or angel who can restrain this. Only Divinity can—and has been doing so for some 2000 years.

(6) There is no other satisfactory explanation. Some have contended that the restraining One is Human Government, and yet, in this case, the Antichrist is the government; he will certainly not restrain himself. Some have suggested Michael the archangel, yet Michael's primary function is to protect Israel during the reign of Antichrist, not to prevent Antichrist from reigning.

We understand from Daniel and Revelation that the reign of Antichrist, as the head of a ten nation confederacy, BEGINS with the institution of a seven year covenant of peace between Israel and the nations around her (Dan. 9:27). This means that the Holy Spirit's removal and the Rapture of the Church will take place prior to that seven year covenant of peace. Antichrist will then deceive the world through mighty signs and cause peace and craft to prosper. In the midst of that seven year period, Antichrist will break the covenant and the Great Tribulation will begin.

REASON NO. IX

The Threefold Order of the Resurrection of the Righteous

In that great resurrection chapter of 1 Corinthians 15, the apostle Paul gives us crucial information about the "order[s]" (verse 23) of the resurrection of the righteous. Unlike the singular resurrection of the wicked, there are different groups or companies in the resurrection of the righteous. This means that the resurrection of the saints will not happen all at once. There are different specific stages to it. This also means that the resurrection of the Old Testament saints takes place at a different time and "order" than that of the Church saints. This is perfectly consistent with all the facts presented as proof of the pretribulational Rapture of the Church of Jesus Christ. In verse 20 of this chapter Paul gave us the first signal concerning these "orders." He said, "But now Christ has been raised up from the dead, the '**firstfruit**' of those who have fallen asleep."

This word "firstfruit" tells us that Paul was going back to the Harvest Feasts of Israel, as given in the Hebrew Scriptures, to use them as a pattern for the resurrection of the righteous dead. When we look back at the Law of Moses we find that there were three Feasts centered around the harvest theme. On these three occasions all the men of Israel were required to appear before God in Jerusalem for the solemn observance of these three Feasts (Exo.23:14–17). Let us note each one.

First, at the Feast of Unleavened Bread (Passover) there was the actual waving up in the air of a "sheaf" or handful of the early green ears of grain. This was said to be the "firstfruit" of grain which was dedicated to God and used as a token of the greater spring harvest to be celebrated 50 days later (Lev. 23:9–14).

Second, there was the Feast of Firstfruits (or of Weeks, since they counted seven weeks). In the Greek Scriptures this is called Pentecost (meaning 50th). On this occasion they were to grind up some of the harvested grain and make two loaves of bread. These two loaves were to be waved up in the air just like the bundle of grain which was waved up 50 days earlier (Lev. 23:15–21).

Third and last, there was the final harvest Feast at the "end of the year," which was the fall harvest festival of "Ingathering," sometimes called "Tabernacles" (Lev. 23:33–36).

Next, in verse 22 of this chapter Paul told us that this resurrection of which he was speaking has to do with those who are "in Christ"—"*In Christ shall all be made alive.*" The unsaved are never said to be "in Christ." In every case where Paul used this expression, especially in this chapter, he meant the saints—see verses 18, 19, 22, 31 and 58. As to the resurrection of those "in Christ," Paul says in verse 23 the very important words—

"But each in his own **order:**"

W.E. Vine gives the standard meaning of the word "order." "That which is arranged in order, was especially a military term, denoting a company; it is used metaphorically in 1 Corinthians 15:23 of the various classes of those who have part in the first resurrection." Then Paul gives the various "orders" or companies in the resurrection of the righteous.

(1) (First,)   "Christ the firstfruits,"
(2) "afterward (epeita-next in sequence) those who are Christs' at His coming."
(3) "then (eita-next in sequence)   the end, . . . when death is destroyed."

Thus, we have three "orders" in the resurrection of the righteous. This is obviously in keeping with the three Feasts of Israel as previously stated. It is important to remember, in sequences such as this, that the subjects of the sequence must remain in the same nature or character. All three of these "Orders" have to do with the resurrection of the righteous.

(1) The first order is self-explanatory. Jesus Christ is the "firstfruit" of the righteous dead.
(2) The second order are those who "are Christ's." This means they belong to Christ. Christ is the "Firstfruit" or sample of the spring harvest called "Firstfruits" or Pentecost. Christ is the token and guarantee of what is to come at harvest. In another great resurrection chapter of Romans 8, the apostle Paul identified believers today—that is, the Church—as those who "have the *firstfruits* of the Spirit, waiting for the *redemption of our bodies*" (v. 23). That means that the second order in this sequence is the Church of Jesus Christ. The Holy Spirit already confirmed this to us because the Church was born on the Feast Day of "Firstfruits" or Pentecost, signifying the Church's vital connection to what is symbolized in that Feast day. We can be sure that the meaning of this Feast day and its particular offering lay dormant in Israel's history until the time of the particular revelations given to the apostle Paul.
(3) This leaves the resurrection of all the Old Testament saints and the Tribulation saints who were killed. They are symbolized by the final harvest Feast of "Ingathering" or "Tabernacles." This was done at the "end" (Exo. 23:16) of the year and the resurrection of

the Old Testament saints was said to be at "the end" of days, or at the "end" of the age (Dan. 12:1–3, 13; John 11:24). Likewise, the special law regarding "gleanings" at the end of the harvest (Lev. 23:22 and Deut. 24:19–22) could be a picture of the resurrection of the Tribulation saints. Please remember that all the passages which were given in "REASON No. I" apply to this third resurrection "order." And, as I pointed out before, they leave out the Rapture of the Church. Interestingly enough, at this harvest Feast there is no special offering like the "Wave-sheaf" or "Wave-loaves" which symbolized the ascension of Christ and the Church. The resurrected in this case go right into the Millennial Kingdom on earth.

Thus we have the three orders of the resurrection of the righteous:

(1) Christ, *Firstfruits sample*—Wave-sheaf
(2) Church, *Harvest of Firstfruits*—Wave-loaves
(3) Old Testament and Tribulation Saints, *Harvest of Ingathering and Gleanings*

Deuteronomy 16:1–17 recapitulates the Feasts with the added command of "rejoicing" for the Feast of Weeks (Pentecost) and the Feast of Ingathering or Tabernacles. This beautifully represents the great happiness and rejoicing which will take place for us at the Rapture—"For what is our hope, or joy, or crown of *rejoicing* ? Are not even ye in the presence of our Lord Jesus Christ at His coming? For ye are our glory and joy." (1 Thess. 2:19, 20).

REASON NO. X

The Problem of Who Will Furnish the Kingdom— If Both Events Happen Simultaneously

If the Rapture of the Church happens at the very same time Christ returns to destroy the wicked and rule on earth, then there are real problems. If the righteous are caught up and the wicked are damned, who will be left alive on earth to furnish or go into the Millennial Kingdom? This is no little problem with which every teacher, who believes that both events happen at the same time, has wrestled. The following are some of the efforts made to accommodate or work around this problem.

First, there are "post and amillennialists" who deny that there is a future literal Kingdom reign of Christ. They teach that "the Church is the Kingdom" and therefore, at the coming of Christ, the saved are taken to heaven and the wicked are all damned at the same time. The problem with this position is obvious. The Bible clearly reveals that the Church is not the prophesied Messianic Kingdom, and Christ will indeed reign on earth for 1000 years (Rev. 20:2, 3, 4, 5, 6, 7).

Second, there are those like the Seventh Day Adventists who realize that if all happens at the same time there would be no one left on earth. Yet they also realize that there is a 1000 year time period on earth clearly revealed. Thus, they teach that the earth will actually be empty and desolate (except for Satan) for one thousand years. They are at least consistent. The problem with this position is that they deny the clear revelation that Christ will reign on earth amongst the redeemed out of the Tribulation on a glorious earth, not a desolate earth.

Third, there are those like the Watchtower Society and Herbert W. Armstrong who argue that there is really no such thing as the Rapture of the Church. They say it is just figurative language, which means that living saints all go alive into the Millennial Kingdom on earth. The problem with this position is that there is clear revelation that the Rapture is literal and just as real as the Judgment of the lost and the Kingdom Age, itself.

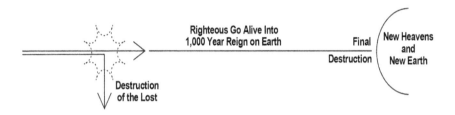

Fourth, there are "posttribulational" fundamentalists who congest everything into a singular (or near singular) event. They say it must all happen at or about the same time. There are as many variations of this as there are proponents, because it very obviously has problems and contradictions, very much like a mad traffic jam! Trying to get the Church caught up to meet Christ at the second coming and yet returning with Him to reign, and at the very same time destroying the unbelievers—yet somehow saving some of them—but not rapturing them with the rest, is no little task.

This fourth position ignores the clear revelation that the saints who endure through the reign of Antichrist and the Great Tribulation go alive into the Millennial Kingdom to repopulate the earth. At the second coming of Christ, He will "gather all nations" and separate the sheep from the goats (Matt. 25:31–33). If the Rapture had already just taken place as depicted above, there would be no need for another separation. It would have already happened!

The truth and absolute necessity of the matter is that the Rapture of the Church and the second coming of Christ to judge and reign are two separate events with the reign of Antichrist in between them.

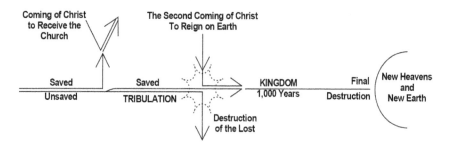

THE FIVE CONFLICTS
(Reasons XI–XV)

REASON NO. XI

The Conflict of Economies

Though there was a clear transition in the early Church in the book of Acts, out of Judaism into pure Christianity, there is no such transition revealed for the close of this Age or in the Great Tribulation. Looking into the prophecies of the Tribulation period, we find that the Law of Moses and Temple worship are clearly practiced by the saints. If the Church exists until the coming of Christ to reign, then all the saved will be in the Church and they are clearly forbidden (by the revelations given to Paul) to practice the Law (Eph. 2:13–15; Col. 2:14–16; 2 Cor. 3:7–11; Heb. 8:13, etc). Today, both saved Jews and Gentiles spiritually lose their national identity and are jointly placed into "one body," also called "one new man." Such is not the case of believers in the Tribulation period. Therefore, there is created by this false teaching a great conflict of economies.

Who or what should the saints obey? However, when the Church is Raptured, there is obviously an abrupt termination of "the Law of Christ" (1 Cor. 9:21 and Rom. 8:2) for the Church. Therefore, those who are saved in the Tribulation period are consistently free to practice the Law system in anticipation of Christ's New Covenant Kingdom reign.

REASON NO. XII

The Conflict of Buildings

Today, in this Age of Grace, God is actively building a Holy Temple (Eph. 2:19–22). This Temple is spiritual in nature. It is made of living stones. Its foundation is Christ. All saints should be actively engaged in this building program as instructed by Paul, "as a wise master builder, I have laid the foundation [by distinctive revelations] . . . but let every man take heed how he builds there upon" (1 Cor. 3:10). Both Jews and Gentiles who are saved today are jointly engaged in this building program. "For we are the circumcision, who worship God in spirit, rejoice in Christ Jesus, and have no confidence in the flesh" (Philip. 3:3). The physical Temple was destroyed. The Head of the Church in heaven is not interested in issuing any other "building permits" during this Age of Grace. However, in the Tribulation period, the physical *"Temple of God"* in Jerusalem will once again be functioning and will be the center of the world's attention. This surely indicates that the present building program has terminated and a totally different economy and building program has begun.

REASON NO. XIII

The Conflict of Hopes

Everything about the blessed hope of the Church is heavenly in nature (see John 14:1–3; 1 Thess. 1:10; 2:19; 3:13; 4:13–18; Eph.

1:3, 18; 4:4, 30; 5:27; Philip. 1:6, 10; 2:16; 3: 11–12; 3: 20–21; 4:5; Col. 1:5, 21–23, 27–28; 3:4; 2 Tim. 4:8; Titus 2:13, etc.). This hope is centered around Jesus Christ Who will take us into heavenly glory. It has nothing whatsoever to do with which political party is running for office, or what the nations of earth are doing for the pitiful plight of world conditions. All these things are of serious concern, but none of them have anything whatsoever to do with the hope of the Church—the true Church, the "body of Christ."

In contrast to this, the hope of Israel does center around government and world conditions. Their hope is in the Messiah Who will bring in a perfect rule on earth. "The desert will blossom as a rose," "the nations will beat their swords into plowshares," and "the knowledge of the Lord will be from sea to sea." Many are the prophecies of the Messiah ruling with "a rod of iron" over the whole earth.

Now, if we have both these hopes represented by two different groups of preachers evangelizing the world at the same time, with both groups claiming to represent God's message for the last generation and telling the world what to hope for, we are really going to have confusion! Nobody will know which to believe in or hope for! Those evangelizing for Israel will say, "Forget about heaven; our hope is in the Messiah coming to restore this earth!" Those evangelizing for the body of Christ will say, "Forget about this earth and all its problems; our hope is in heaven from whence we look for our Savior!"

This is precisely why dispensational distinctions are so very important.

REASON NO. XIV

The Conflict of "Grace" versus "Wrath"

God is appealing to the world today on the basis of His "grace" (see John 1:17; Rom. 5:2; 6:14; Gal. 5:4, etc.). Today God's *grace* is said to be "reigning" (Rom.5:21). God is drawing the attention of the world to the redemption provided for mankind in the substitutionary death, burial and resurrection of Christ. God is likewise appealing to the Church to live under the principles manifested through the *grace* of God in Christ. God is saying to earth, "Look at what blessed graces I have provided for you in Christ"—eternal redemption, everlasting life and victory over sin in living. This is why this Age is called "the Dispensation of the Grace of God" (Eph. 3:2). What characterizes this Age is the manifestation of the gospel of the grace of God.

In vivid contrast to this is the fact that when one opens the pages of divine revelation concerning the Great Tribulation time period, he looks WRATH square in the face. The vicious eyes and snarling teeth of *wrath* are on every page, shredding the world to pieces. There is absolutely nothing in all human history as foreboding as the coming time when the earth will wallow in its pain and suffering. The book of Revelation is frightening. God is speaking to the world in His *wrath* in the pages of the book of Revelation. That is the primary and fundamental message during the reign of rebellion under Antichrist.

Pretribulationalists do not say that God's salvation grace is not available in the Great Tribulation, for it is. Nor do they say that there are not episodes of disaster in this Age of Grace, for there are. But what I am saying is that these two time periods are in characteristic contrast; they do not go together, nor can they overlap.

REASON NO. XV

The Conflict of Reigns

As I have already stated under "REASON No. VIII, (2)," the free reign of Antichrist, both politically and ideologically in wickedness, cannot coexist with the reign of the Holy Spirit in righteousness. The reign of the "*Holy*" Spirit on earth, embodied in the "new creation," could not be simultaneous with the reign of the "*un-holy*" spirit (Lucifer), embodied in the "Man of Sin."

In 2 Corinthians 3:7–9, the word used in Greek for "ministration" is *diakonia,* which is the noun form of the verb *diakoneo*. The verb form signifies a minister serving, whereas the noun form signifies the particular office or ministration of the servant or the organization. In the Revised Version it is properly and literally translated "ministration" (sometimes in the Authorized Version—"administration"). In 2 Corinthians 3:7–9 we read that the present "ministration of the Spirit" is held up in contrast to the "ministration" of the Law of Moses. In the same passage the inspired apostle Paul tells us that the Holy Spirit's rule is a "ministration of righteousness." Thus, the Holy Spirit's presence on earth stands in direct restraint to the spirit of "lawlessness."

When the Holy Spirit came to reside on earth, there was a veritable explosion of spiritual testimony before the world. It seems as if Christianity conquered the whole Roman empire within a few hundred years. Only when the reign of the Holy Spirit ceases, can the "Man of Lawlessness" be revealed and function in a "revived Roman empire" under his control. It even appears in the Scriptures that the Antichrist will be the world's overwhelming choice of a "savior." Such worldwide deception could only take place by the withdrawal of that powerful ministration of the Holy Spirit of God.

THE FIVE CONFIRMATIONS in the Great Tribulation
(Reasons XVI–XX)

REASON NO. XVI

The Great Tribulation Is Jewish in Nature— Not Church-Oriented

The Great Tribulation is a time period wherein God will again be dealing with Israel and the Jewish people.

(1) "70 weeks [of Years] determined upon [Israel] and the Holy City" (Dan. 9:24).
(2) The center of world attention will be "the Holy Place" where Antichrist will dwell (2 Thess. 2:4).
(3) Antichrist will enter "the Temple," claiming to be god (2 Thess. 2:4; Dan. 11:31 and 12:11).

(4) There are special instructions for those in Judea (Matt.24:16).
(5) There will be the observance of the Jewish Sabbath day (Matt.24:20).
(6) "Sacrifice and Oblations" will again be practiced (Dan. 9:27; 8:11–14).
(7) The 12 Tribes of Israel will again have clear representation (Rev. 7 and 14).
(8) The "two witnesses" will exercise the spirit and power of Moses and Elijah (Rev. 11:3–12 and Luke 9:30).
(9) Both the outer court of the Temple and the City of Jerusalem will be occupied by enemies (Rev. 11:1, 2).
(10) The Tribulation will be upon Daniel's people (Dan. 9:24; 12:1, etc.).
(11) The "Gospel of the Kingdom" will again be preached (Matt.24:14).
(12) Elijah will come to turn the hearts of fathers and sons (Matt. 17:11 and Mal.4:5, 6).

REASON NO. XVII

The Great Tribulation "Saints" are Not Church Saints

Much is said in the books of Daniel, Matthew and Revelation about the "saints" of God who will live and do battle with the Antichrist. These saints dwell on earth and are under the final world system, but they will put their trust in God and not submit to Antichrist's number or blasphemy. Even though at first the Antichrist and his forces will prevail against them, yet they do not surrender their allegiance to God. Eventually they will overcome Antichrist "by the blood of the Lamb and the word of their testimony." In Daniel chapter 7, verse 21, the Antichrist "wars against the saints" and prevails. Again it says, "he wears out the saints" (v. 25), yet the saints shall take the Kingdom and possess it (vs. 18 and 22). It will be God's favor to give the saints the Kingdom (v. 27). In Revelation (6:9–11) many saints will be martyred because of the Word of God and their testimony. In Rev. 12:11 the saints "overcome by the blood of the lamb and their testimony." In Rev. 15:2–4, the saints are the final victors.

As we have already stated earlier in "REASON No. III," in Matthew 3, 13, 24 and 25 following the Tribulation, the saints are gathered into the Kingdom after serving God during the "seven" year time of their calling and severe trials. Obviously, since none of these saints are ever said to be Church saints, and are never said to be collectively raptured into heaven, it is confirmation that the Church is not present.

REASON NO. XVIII

The Great Tribulation is the "Time of Jacob's Trouble," Not the Church's Trouble

One of the purposes of the Great Tribulation is illustrated for us in the story of Joseph and his brethren. Many years after Joseph had been rejected by his brethren and sold to the Gentiles, he became a great ruler in Egypt. When an unprecedented seven year period of severe famine came upon the world, his brethren come to Egypt for help and relief. They did not recognize their brother, Joseph, but he recognized them. Joseph treated his brethren very harshly, even though he also helped them. The severity of Joseph's dealing with his brethren brought them to a place where they reflected back in their guilty consciences to the evil deed they had done to Joseph. They finally arrived at an attitude of heart where Joseph could openly receive and bless them. The story is very emotional, but it beautifully illustrates how God will deal with His people during the Great Tribulation which will come upon the world in the last days. God will use it to bring Israel to Himself.

In Jeremiah 30:4–9 the inspired prophet says of that final time, "Alas! for that day is great, so that none is like it: it is even the TIME OF JACOB'S TROUBLE; but he shall be saved out of it."

In Ezekiel 20:33–38, the prophet speaks of that time in these words, "And I will bring you out from the people . . . where you are scattered . . . with fury poured out. And I will bring you into the wilderness of the people, and THERE WILL I PLEAD MY CASE WITH YOU FACE TO FACE . . . and I will cause you to pass under the rod . . . and I will purge out from among you the rebels."

In Matthew 24:15–22 and Luke 21:23 Christ speaks of the Great Tribulation and the nation of Israel, saying, "there will be great wrath upon this people."

In Zechariah 13:8 and 9, the prophet speaks of that time, "And it shall come to pass in all the land, says the LORD, 'That two-thirds in it shall be cut off and die. But one-third shall be left in it: I will bring the one-third through the fire, will refine them as silver is refined, and test them as gold is tested. They will call on My Name, and I will answer them. I will say, "This is My people"; and each one will say, The LORD is my God.'"

REASON NO. XIX

In the Great Tribulation, the "Woman" of God's Favor is Israel, Not the Church

May I say it reverently, "God is not a polygamist!" The Scriptures bear out that God has on earth only ONE "Woman" at a time! It is well-known by all Bible students that in the Hebrew Scriptures God speaks by metaphor or analogy that the nation of Israel is "the wife of Jehovah." When Israel departed from God in idolatry, the prophets likened it to "Israel's playing the harlot," and God said He would "divorce" His wife (Hosea 2:2; Isa. 50:1). Yet, God also promised that in the latter days He would bring her to Himself once again. (As examples of this see — Ezek. 16:8–63; Hosea 2:2, 16 and 19).

In the interim during Israel's present departure, Christ, by a similar metaphor, has likened the Church which is His Body to His bride, who will be "presented to Him" in Heaven as "a chaste virgin" (Eph. 5:21–33; 2 Cor. 11:2 and 3). This Woman is not found in the Hebrew Scriptures or the book of Revelation.

Who, then, is the *"Woman"* of God's favor in the book of Revelation chapter 12 during the Great Tribulation? It is not at all difficult to identify her. In verse 1 she has "a crown of twelve stars"; this speaks of twelve tribe Israel. In verse 5 "she brought forth a Man Child Who was to rule all nations"—Israel, who gave to us the Lord Jesus Christ. In the Great Tribulation, Satan will "persecute the Woman who brought forth the Man Child" (again, Israel is in view). Finally, God will supernaturally protect the Woman (verses 14–17), even though Satan "makes war against the remnant of her [Israel's] seed." The final "Marriage Supper of the Lamb" takes place at the end of the Great Tribulation (see Psalm 45:1–17; Matt. 22:1–14; 25:1–13 and Rev. 19:7–10). Israel is primarily in view.

REASON NO. XX

The Great Tribulation Spells the Doom of Apostate Christendom

And it is Appropriate that the "Body of Christ" not be Present

The antithesis to the "Mystery Body of Christ," as seen in Paul's letters, is shockingly displayed in the book of Revelation as "Mystery Babylon, that old whore, the mother of harlots and abominations of earth" (Rev. 17 and 18). Yes, the final form of apostate Christendom is "Mystery Babylon the Great." Most evangelical Christians recognize this fact. However, perhaps the strongest argument that this is Roman Catholicism (and her Protestant daughters) is from the footnotes in the Roman Catholic Bible, itself. There they admit that the city is "Rome." They further admit that "pagan religion" is in view. However, they dodge the implication of a reference to their paganism by saying that this is "the past pagan religion" of Rome (see the footnotes in The Douay Version, or The New American Bible, etc.). The only problem with this explanation is that the account in Revelation is a *prophecy of the future* Great Tribulation just prior to the second coming of Christ. So it is *future* pagan Rome—not the past pagan Rome—that is in view! And the future pagan Rome, richly decorated and jeweled, is sitting over there on the Tiber River right NOW awaiting the fulfillment of this prophecy.

When Jesus Christ was rejected and crucified by His own people, the Law Dispensation was terminated, a new Age began, and shortly thereafter the horrible destruction of Jerusalem took place by the powerful Roman armies. And so it will be, that as apostate Christendom has totally rejected Christ as the living Head and has occasioned the Holocaust of the physical brethren of Christ (the Jews), the Age of Grace will be terminated, the Tribulation will begin, and shortly thereafter the horrible destruction of "Mystery Babylon" will take place by the same Roman power—the restored Roman Empire of the last days. Notice the chart below.

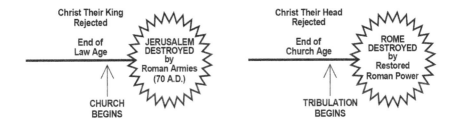

In conclusion, it can be added:

(1) No one actually believes that the "Church which is Christ's Body" will go through the Great Tribulation. This may *sound* as a very surprising statement to make! Why do I make it?? Because it is a fact that as the corporate collective "body of Christ," beginning from Pentecost until the Rapture, "the Church" could not possibly go through the Great Tribulation. At best, only the last generation of believers in this Church Age would be able to do so. Therefore, the collective "body of Christ" will not go through the time period of "the Great Tribulation."

(2) Furthermore, the Great Tribulation Scriptural passages never mention "the Church which is Christ's body" in any passage or book and there is *no revealed purpose* for the Church being there!

Jack W. Langford
P.O. Box 801, Joshua, TX 76058
817-295-6454
www.SeparationTruth.com
langfordjw@sbcglobal.net

CPSIA information can be obtained
at www.ICGtesting.com
Printed in the USA
LVHW042241020520
654898LV00007B/1080